Tender Truths

DONATED BY OLGA NIKOLAJEV RN, MA, FT
END OF LIFE NURSE EDUCATOR
DYINGMATTERS.CA

IROQUOIS, ONTARIO, CANADA

Also in the Caring for the Dying Series

Bold Spirit Caring for the Dying

and

Bold Spirit Gratitude Journal

Tender Truths
Caring for the Dying

TAMELYNDA LUX

Patti Broadfoot * Brenda Hennessey
Olga Nikolajev * Chrystal Waban * Rusty Williams

TENDER TRUTHS CARING FOR THE DYING

Patti Broadfoot, Brenda Hennessey, Tamelynda Lux

Olga Nikolajev, Chrystal Waban, Rusty Williams

Copyright © 2022 **Bold Spirit Press**

Lux & Associates / Tamelynda Lux

All Right Reserved. No part of this publication may be reproduced, distributed, or transmitted in any form or by any means, including but not limited to photocopying, recording, or other electronic or mechanical methods without the prior written permission from the lead author, Tamelynda Lux, except in the case of brief quotations embodied in critical reviews and certain non-commercial uses permitted by copyright law.

Neither the author nor co-authors nor the publisher can be held responsible for any loss, claim, or damage arising out of the use, or misuse, of the suggestions made, the failure to take medical advice, or for any material on third-party websites.

The stories in this book are all true, but to ensure anonymity and protect privacy, some identifying names have been changed. Details that are specific to a client, patient, or loved one may have been altered as well. Permissions have been obtained for those stories where identifying names and details have not been changed.

First Printing: 2022

Bold Spirit Press

Copyright © 2022 Bold Spirit Press / Tamelynda Lux / Lux & Associates

All rights reserved.

ISBN Print Book: 978-0-9940927-8-6

WHAT OTHERS ARE SAYING

"I wish I'd had the wisdom of this book when I was accompanying my mom in her dying. While it is particularly relevant for practitioners and caregivers working with the dying, it is appropriate for anyone who has an aging parent, friend, or a partner with a terminal illness—which, at some point, will be almost all of us. The more we can talk about death, as the writers of this book have learned, the more we can understand and appreciate our own lives."

~ Heather Plett, Author of *The Art of Holding Space:*
A Practice of Love, Liberation, and Leadership and
Co-founder of the Centre for Holding Space

☙❧

"*Tender Truths Caring for the Dying* is an excellent resource for those who support the dying. But the book is not tender in a soft, fragile way. The authors share honest, experience-based reflections. Their combined words offer readers essential, accessible, and, yes, tender tools for all who help support the dying: deeper knowledge, the value of self-reflection, and an emphasis on vulnerability."

~ Larry Patten, Author of *A Companion for the Hospice Journey*

"*Tender Truths Caring for the Dying* is a must-read that helps us connect to our own vulnerability around death, which can open up healing for others. Olga [Nikolajev] demystifies death and dying while incorporating a holistic approach. Along with the physical, incorporating the psychosocial and spiritual aspects provides the ability for the dying person to be empowered in their living. Olga's down-to-earth approach guides us to acknowledge that death and the dying process are natural, relational, and holistic. We can better understand some of the pains, discomforts, and uneasiness we may experience as we care for those dying and grieving and approach death ourselves."

~ Yvette Murray, Mental Health Speaker and Advocate, MentalHealthTrainer.ca

꿍ꥹ

"Patti [Broadfoot] has been able to shine a beautifully compassionate light on the reality that all behavior has meaning. It takes a special person like Patti to honor that and endeavor to find meaning in each unique circumstance.

"A favorite passage is, 'As caregivers, our toolbox of thoughts and ideas must be diverse.' This is an incredibly important point and not always easy to hold true to as we often want to 'fix things' in our own way. Patti teaches us throughout her piece that we need to be fully present and listen keenly and allow those we serve to lead the way.

"As an end-of-life doula, I am very grateful to have Patti's perspective on behaviors. I will be more mindful in my work, allowing myself the time to investigate actions that are typically out of place for someone.

"I look forward to learning from each author in *Tender Truths Caring for the Dying* and extend my thanks."

~ Sue Phillips, Critical Illness/End-of-Life Doula, and Funeral Celebrant

"As an ordained minister and a former hospice chaplain, I applaud a book that covers the much-needed discussion on the process of dying and death. For many, it is a taboo subject, and when they are abruptly confronted with their own or a loved one dying, they are unprepared. I can particularly relate to Rusty Williams' discussion of the power of presence. In the past, I believed there must be some formula for the correct words to say, only to find that often silent, companionable presence was what was most needed and deeply appreciated. The experiences and thoughts in this book will surely be welcome guidance and affirmation for those facing the dying process."

~ The Rev. Dr. Virginia Leopold, M.Ed., M.Div., Th.M., D.Min.

ಸಂಧ್

"While this book is written for the end-of-life caregiver, anyone can read from it and benefit. The authors comprise a panel of well-educated and highly experienced practitioners. Beautifully written with astonishing and relatable stories, these tales turn the focus onto the practitioner. Through the reading, the book challenges those professionals (and lay persons in the case of their own family or friends) on how to be sincere with themselves as they face their patients' impending death. Practitioners are challenged to consider what that means for their own lives and for their practice.

"This collection also clearly and concisely addresses common concerns and issues. The book's format cleverly utilizes journaling sections and incisive questions for discussion, with answers provided by the co-authors.

"I highly recommend this book for every human being to help us live life joyously and to accept its inevitable end with the dignity and profundity that passage deserves."

~ Jayne M. Wesler, Attorney, LCSW, Author,
Life Coach, Family Caregiver

"Patti [Broadfoot] does an amazing job of coloring the grief experience in an array not yet seen before. She takes us into the heart and soul of the dying, showing us the importance of listening and respecting both the transition and the human. Patti then gives us a glimpse into what is required of her on every level in her line of work. She beautifully explores the topics of balance, accountability, and imposter syndrome. The insightful words placed across these pages need to be seen by those who have experienced grief. Please share it with caregivers and those who work in the field of end of life as well. Her words are light, positive, and uplifting. This is an honest account of her life as a registered social worker and death doula, and I hope you let it inspire you as it did me."

~ Christine E. Cosgrove, BA, RP,
Author of *Born Into Chaos: How I Broke a Generational Cycle of Abuse*

ଛଠ

"This will be a resource I will turn to time and time again. *Tender Truths Caring for the Dying* was written in a way that made me feel as though I was having a conversation with each Author. Relatable stories, practical tips, strategies, and an invitation to reflect at the end of each chapter, means the authors have a deep understanding of the needs of practitioners as we support our clients. Thank you to each author for your insight and the ways in which you showed vulnerability in your writing. On a personal note, thank you to Patti Broadfoot for talking about such important issues as imposter syndrome, the importance of reflective practice, and burnout. You always have a way of shining a light on important topics compassionately and professionally."

~ Joanne Nancekivell, Social Worker,
Committee Member of London Middlesex
Hospice Palliative Care Refresher Day

"Olga Nikolajev has approached the difficult subject of truths about dying with a balance of honesty and compassion, a testament to the terminology of the chapter title: Tender Truths of Death and Dying. Her gentle writing style seamlessly weaves personal and professional experiences with factual information about the holistic nature of dying and the experience of those who companion and bear witness to the process. I was easily drawn into her pattern of writing, with each paragraph pulling me forward with a desire to discover more."

~ Jolene Formaini, RN, BSN, MA, CT,
Certified in Thanatology: Death, Dying and Bereavement, Credentialing Council Chair for Association for Death Education and Counseling, Retired Hospice Nurse and Bereavement Specialist

೮೧೦೩

"Olga [Nikolajev] offers a reflexive and vulnerable narrative, highlighting the 'tender truth' that death is a natural, relational, and holistic process. An engaging read for all caregivers!"

~ Sherry Smith, Ph.D., FT, Lecturer,
Department of Thanatology, King's University College

DEDICATION

To caregivers everywhere.

You are appreciated, valued, and hold a special place in our hearts.

TABLE OF CONTENTS

Co-Authors xv

Foreword xxi

Introduction xxiii

CHAPTER 1 1

All Behavior Has Meaning – Patti Broadfoot

CHAPTER 2 19

Honoring Sacred Truths of Living and Dying While Indigenous – Chrystal Waban

CHAPTER 3 41

Is It Possible to Pray the Wrong Prayer? – Rusty Williams

CHAPTER 4 67

Doing "Too Much" or "Not Enough?" – Tamelynda Lux

CHAPTER 5 89

Just Breathe – Brenda Hennessey

CHAPTER 6 109

Tender Truths of Dying and Death – Olga Nikolajev

Co-Author Dialogue 137

Contact Information 157

About Tamelynda Lux 159

More About This Book 161

About Bold Spirit Press 163

CO-AUTHORS

Patti Broadfoot, RSW

Patti is an end-of-life social worker, grief counselor, and educator registered with the Ontario College of Social Workers and Social Service Workers. She is also a member of the Ontario and Canadian Association of Social Workers, Bereavement Ontario Network, and the Death Doula Ontario Network. Patti has over twenty-five years of experience working with a diverse clientele of children, adolescents, and adults in healthcare and education. Her area of expertise is in complicated, traumatic death and non-death losses.

Brenda Hennessey, End-of-Life Doula

Brenda resides in a small town in southwestern Ontario. She volunteers at her local residential hospice. Supporting her community is important to Brenda. Being part of a resident's end-of-life journey is an honor and joyous part of her work.

Brenda became an "End-of-Life Doula" in June 2020, completing the certification course through Douglas College. She has since completed palliative care, advanced care planning, MAiD, and grief courses and workshops. Brenda is currently enrolled in the thanatology certificate course through Centennial College. She continues to be an active member of the Death Doula Ontario Network and the Southwestern Ontario Death Doula Network.

Tamelynda Lux, CCH, PCC, DipAdEd

With over 30 years of experience, Tamelynda has invested her career in supporting individuals as a life coach and then evolved her private practice to include hypnosis for life issues and concerns, end-of-life support, and grief coaching.

Certified in the specialty of end-of-life hypnosis and as an end-of-life doula, Tamelynda provides non-medical, holistic support to the dying person and/or their family. She is a certified end-of-life doula, certified Psychological First Aid trainer (instructor level) Canadian Red Cross, and has completed Certified Mental Health First Aid with the Canadian Mental Health Association. Tamelynda is actively involved with the aging population, including as a community member on the board of a non-profit for Alzheimer's, dementia, and long-term care.

Olga Nikolajev, RN, MA, FT

Olga Nikolajev is an end-of-life nurse educator, cannabis nurse educator, and end-of-life doula mentor with over twenty-five years of professional experience as a registered nurse in various health care settings, including hospice palliative care.

Olga has been involved in national, provincial, and local community efforts to shift how we view and approach our dying experience, death, and grief. She facilitates courses in thanatology and end-of-life doula across Canada. Olga is the founder and director of Dying Matters, death awareness and educational social enterprise, and the Death Doula Ontario Network, which she founded in June 2020.

CO-AUTHORS

Chrystal Waban Toop, RSSW

Chrystal is a circle keeper, public speaker, doula, counselor, and registered social services worker. Through her mixed Omamiwinini ancestry, Chrystal has reclaimed connections with her traditional community, Pikwakanagan First Nation.

Her heartwork as the Founder of Blackbird Medicines, a grassroots movement that advances healing justice through support from urban and rural First Nations collaborators. Together, they offer several community-led projects, including the Indigenous Death Doula Collective and Endayan Mashkiikii (My Home Medicines).

Rusty Williams, M.Div., D.Min.

Rusty is a police chaplain, a resiliency facilitator for first responders, and a best-selling author. As a former paramedic and retired police detective, he has more than thirty years of experience in emergency services.

As an ordained minister living with a spinal cord tumor, Rusty finds joy in spending time with his pets, allowing him and his wife, Elissa, to share their home in southern New Jersey.

"At the very heart of companioning, is the need to acknowledge each other as equals, not as 'therapist' and 'patient.' What makes us all equals is that we are all human beings who will come to know the pain and suffering that emanates from the loss of those we have loved. We also need each other."

Alan D. Wolfelt, Ph.D., *Companioning the Bereaved*

FOREWORD

"When we journey with someone on their end-of-life path, we often encounter something unexpected, ourselves. Caregiving is a profound exercise in learning about our own needs, hopes, and fears. In your hands is a powerful collection of stories and wisdom that will help you glean the gems of insight and the sacred implicit in this calling."

Michael Hebb
Founder of Death Over Dinner and Author of
Let's Talk about Death (over Dinner):
An Invitation and Guide to Life's Most Important Conversation

INTRODUCTION

One might expect that a book called "Tender Truths Caring for the Dying" would focus on one of the many debates in medical ethics, such as telling a patient the truth about their health, especially when that means giving them bad news. Being sincere when communicating with a patient still appears to be extremely complicated for healthcare professionals; this is documented in numerous journal articles easily found on PubMed (for example, *Assessing effective physician-patient communication skills: "Are you listening to me, doc?"*).

This book is actually about the tender truths that practitioners have faced, mostly about *themselves* while caring for the dying. This is important because, as new end-of-life practitioners, it can be helpful to know how other practitioners are coping. These stories can help you navigate your own experiences by walking you through common concerns and issues.

How complicated or challenging is it for practitioners or caregivers to be sincere with *themselves* and *their feelings* when caring for the dying? The benefits of being sincere with oneself and considering those "tender truths" are self-care and well-being.

We know that end-of-life caregiving is a sensitive topic, and it can be difficult to share with others what we are experiencing as practitioners, so it's essential to have a support system. I am grateful for the support of the Death Doula Ontario Network for the many online evening sessions where we have the opportunity to connect with like-minded peers to share our experiences and heart-wrenching moments. It truly is a community of giving and receiving care, support, and encouragement. And that is how I met these wonderful co-authors.

How This Book Came About

My journey as an end-of-life practitioner began when I received inquiries from clients for support through the stress of caregiving for loved ones with serious illnesses and at the end of life. I tumbled down the rabbit hole of all things end-of-life when I took the first course as an end-of-life doula simply to become better informed. And then, a world of information opened up for me. I was included in conversations that I'd never experienced before, and I was grateful to have many of my questions answered—questions I had not been allowed to discuss with my family.

This book was written because I wanted to know more about practitioners' experiences to better understand what they did, how they felt about their work, and how I could support them. But I wanted to know the real truths—the nitty-gritty ones—about what was going on for clients, patients, their families, and practitioners and caregivers.

These insights were important because, although I had graduated from the college program as an end-of-life doula, I wasn't sure how far into end-of-life caregiving as a practitioner I wanted to go. I knew, however, that the knowledge would serve me in the future with my loved ones.

I have only a little experience caring for loved ones at their end of life, but I have other experience supporting caregivers of those with serious illnesses or dying. Tackling this topic made sense because I'm starting from the beginning as a relatively new end-of-life doula wanting to know everything. With the networks I'm involved in, some

INTRODUCTION

amazing veteran and new practitioners are open and willing to share their experiences in a book, not just for me to read but for the world!

There are lots of wonderful books on the subject of end-of-life. This book even examines our thoughts on one of the celebrated books by Dr. Alan Wolfelt.

Each author was interviewed to gain their insights as they related to Dr. Alan Wolfelt's model tenets of companioning the bereaved from his book *Companioning the Bereaved*. Dr. Wolfelt is recognized as one of North America's leading death educators and grief counselors. He founded the Center for Loss & Life Transition and sold more than a million copies of his books on death and grief worldwide.

For the interviews with our co-authors, I chose to focus on the tenets of companioning the bereaved because they relate so well to caring for the dying. They relate to the individual dying. They relate to their family and friend caregivers. And they relate to their end-of-life and medical caregivers. Grieving isn't just for the living; the dying also grieve and mourn.

We love getting our hands on anything related to end-of-life that will assist us in helping our clients. And so, each author has recommended a book that has impacted them either personally or professionally. There are so many wonderful books on end-of-life caregiving, and these specific recommendations may help you choose which book to next pick up and explore.

The authors were requested to ask a question for co-author discussion. Those questions and the answers have been included. The purpose behind this was to demonstrate how peer mentoring is easy. Each of the answers could be delved into deeper by asking probing questions in a coaching style. Dialogue is important because from the stories and experiences shared, and we can each draw our own conclusions from the various perspectives of our peers.

There is a new component in this book that the first book *Bold Spirit Caring for the Dying*, didn't have: a journaling section at the end of each chapter. This is included for each chapter so you can immediately capture your thoughts on paper. The benefit of journaling is that by grabbing your initial thoughts without judgment and writing them down immediately, you may find other areas to dive deeper into and explore. Feel free to contact any of the authors or me if you wish to have a deeper conversation. We are here to help so that you know you are not alone in your journey as an end-of-life practitioner. **info@TenderTruthsCaringForTheDying.com**

End-of-life caregiving is a sensitive topic, and yet you have picked up this book because you have likely embarked on a career as either a full-time or part-time end-of-life practitioner or a caregiver. The stories and perspectives you will read in this book come from our experiences of finding or being confronted by tender truths. I hope you find your own tender truths in the experiences so generously shared by the authors.

As you read, keep an open heart and mind to allow for new perspectives to perhaps flutter like butterflies. These butterflies of perspectives can bring awareness so that when you come across a similar but likely unique situation, you will recall how another end-of-life practitioner experienced it. Whether it's right or wrong for you, it can give you at least some foundation on which you can grow. It's important and beneficial to be prepared for the unexpected and be ready for whatever it brings.

As one of my mentors says, "Take what works and leave the rest." But I trust there will be lots for you to embrace and take with you as you journey along in your very important role as an end-of-life practitioner or caregiver.

INTRODUCTION

I will be forever grateful to Patti, Brenda, Olga, Chrystal, and Rusty for contributing to this book because I know there has been a lot going on in each and every one of their lives. And yet these passionate individuals, whom I call friends, give of themselves openly to help others in their roles as practitioners or caregivers.

Tamelynda Lux

**"Writing down our stories gives voice to the importance of
end-of-life care. Sharing them offers the gift of hope."**

Tamelynda Lux, Founder, Bold Spirit Press

CHAPTER 1

ALL BEHAVIOR HAS MEANING
Patti Broadfoot

> "Be the change you wish to see in the world."
> ~ Mahatma Gandhi

Ron cried out endlessly day and night in unmanageable writhing pain. It seemed nothing could alleviate his suffering. Our interdisciplinary team members, his friends and family, and anyone remotely connected to caring for Ron were all baffled and deeply upset by what was happening to him. The images of Ron's suffering repeatedly played in my head day and night, at work, at home, and especially when trying to sleep. I could not make sense of the extreme unmanageable pain. The disease slowly ending his life did not typically produce such severe, uncontrollable pain. So why was the pain medication not working?

Additionally, Ron had started developing some odd behaviors. Usually a soft-spoken, kind-hearted man, Ron had become angry, short-tempered, and combative. Even with or possibly because of his unmanaged pain, Ron would pace endlessly back and forth in his home, constantly fidgeting with menial tasks like rearranging small items around the house. He would randomly mumble, "I should have known something like this would happen." When asked about this comment, Ron just looked at us blankly. I was baffled, and an immense feeling of imposter syndrome quickly took over.

Social work, for me, is a second career. It's one that I chose as an adult and not as an impressionable young teenager. When I was younger, I chose my career based on my parents' guidance, deciding to go into dentistry as my mom worked in the dental field, and to be honest, I didn't think I was smart enough to become what I really wanted—a nurse.

I question if this feeling of not being smart enough as a teenager led me into a massive case of imposter syndrome. I honestly thought I had prepared myself sufficiently for this career in end-of-life care. Passionate about end-of-life care, I was and still am incredibly determined to help other families navigate their journeys better than I had experienced with my family and close friends. My journey began by volunteering at a local hospice. There I learned the practicalities, benevolence, and tenderness of end-of-life care. This work inspired me to return to school—university! Yes, that very thing I thought I wasn't smart enough to do, I did it. I graduated with a social work degree with a minor in thanatology (death and dying). To my surprise, I was on the dean's list every year and graduated with honors.

I thought I was prepared to handle a challenging situation like Ron's, but not being able to help him left me feeling hopeless and doubting myself. Was I really cut out for this career? Maybe I wasn't smart enough after all. I'm now a professional, and I had no idea what was going on or how to help.

It has never been in my nature to give up. Call it my stubborn Scottish heritage. Maybe it is because I have experienced many difficult moments that I worked hard to overcome. I was not disposed to giving up, and I was not about to start now. There had to be a way to figure this out and help Ron. And so, as the saying goes, I pulled myself up by the bootstraps, put imposter syndrome on the shelf, and went to work finding a way to help Ron.

Through my education and training, I knew that end-of-life clients like Ron often lose their ability to communicate effectively, resulting in responsive behaviors. People often express unmet needs, such as thirst, hunger, pain, frustration, loneliness, or boredom, in various ways. I have seen these needs expressed in behaviors such as aggressive outbursts, agitation, wandering, restlessness, paranoia, and depression. I reflected on my Introduction to Psychology course, where I learned about behaviors and their associated responses discovered through Pavlov's bell experiment.

If you are unfamiliar with the story, Pavlov conditioned a dog to salivate and unconsciously associate food with a ringing bell. With Ron, I saw his learned behaviors, but I had no idea what the bell was or what exactly the cause of the behavior was. What was he trying to tell us through his mumblings and unmanageable pain?

Being an effective social worker is not just about gaining an education. Every person you work with is an individual, requiring an individual approach and often outside the academic box way of thinking. As caregivers, our tool belt of thoughts and ideas must be diverse. Many days I feel like a detective. I have learned the importance of following a bread crumb trail of clues and listening to my "spidey senses." By remaining curious about a client's behavior and thinking outside the box, I can usually come up with a plan to help. So, with that in mind and listening to my intuition, I decided to dig deeper into Ron's personal history to gain further insight.

While speaking with Ron's family, I learned he was raised by strict Catholic parents who had hoped and dreamed their son would enter the priesthood. But instead, Ron rebelled and explored many other religions, some vastly different from his Catholic upbringing, such as Buddhism and Hinduism. My detective's brain lit up like a light bulb. I wondered, as Ron was nearing the end of his life, if he was questioning his decision to rebel against his parents' religion. Could an internal emotional battle be a contributing factor to Ron's behavior and increased pain?

To see if my theory about Ron's behavior was correct, and with Ron's permission, a local priest came and spoke with him. It was like magic. After their meeting, Ron's pain significantly subsided, and his pacing and mumblings stopped.

This experience taught me that all behavior has meaning. I just had to get curious and become a detective to discover the meaning of any client's behavior. And more importantly for me, I learned when imposter syndrome pokes its nose into my life, I need to not allow fear to immobilize me. It is better to acknowledge and explore the feelings and remind myself that many others have these moments. I am smart enough. I have the skillset and have access to many amazing people. I can reach out for assistance when I get stuck.

Another client named William also taught me a great deal about behavior having meaning and the importance of not judging a book by its cover. Opposite to Ron, William had historically displayed anger, frequently lashing out at his family and caregivers. And while it was often difficult not to take his actions personally, our team of healthcare workers chalked up his irritating behaviors to "That's just who William is and always will be."

However, there was another truth for me to learn. As you may be aware, as someone nears the end of life, they often go through a form of life review. I will typically help clients explore this process by asking them about stories from their past.

Over a few weeks, William decided that I was a safe enough person to share some of his more profound and darker life stories with. I already knew William had been a prisoner of war as his family had shared this information previously. William had refused to speak about any details of his war experiences to his friends and family. However, over a few weeks in our private sessions, William began to disclose many horrific stories of his time as a soldier and prisoner. It was almost like he needed to unburden himself to finally find peace. I was overwhelmed listening to these stories and experienced intense, overwhelming emotions, horrified at what one human can do to another. I was outraged that he had experienced all these horrific things and felt great sorrow that he could not share his experiences with others and carried such a heavy burden alone over the years.

With every visit learning more stories, my heart ached for a man who had been living in a private, hidden world of self-torture over the past fifty-plus years. I have experienced trauma in my life, but it never came close to the extent that William had, and I couldn't imagine not seeking help to work through the profound thoughts and emotions during this traumatic period of his life.

Upon self-reflection, I realized that I had allowed the judgment of others to obscure my own beliefs about William's behavior and not what was truly going on below the surface. William had suppressed his emotions caused by the atrocities he experienced while a prisoner of war and his actions as a soldier inflicting pain and killing the enemies he faced on the battlefield, which he carried heavily with him throughout life. He explained that he was married to a beautiful wife and was blessed with wonderful children, grandchildren, and even one great-grandchild, and all he could envision throughout what were to be happy times were the men and women whose lives he took on the battlefield. They were people too, just like him. They would never know the joy of a family. How could he have done such horrible things?

Here, in these intimate moments of William sharing his deepest thoughts and feelings, I discovered the importance of suspending judgment of a client's behavior before learning the whole story. How are we to honestly know what they have or are experiencing now? Once again, all behavior has meaning at every stage of our lives. William's behavior resulted from his traumatic life events and the incredible feelings of guilt and anger for the atrocities he experienced as a prisoner and the lives he took on the battlefield.

Working with Ron and William taught me the importance of self-reflective practice when it comes to the client's behavior and my own. On days that I faced more challenging issues, such as listening to William's stories, I noticed that I had a shorter fuse becoming easily angered, frustrated, or utterly physically and mentally exhausted. Caregiving is stressful. This is not something new. Caregiving is one of the most stressful and exhausting jobs, whether as a professional or a family member. I have witnessed fellow team members become very cynical, disengaged, and hopeless—all signs of burnout. Often people view their exhaustion and feeling drained as a normal part of the job. However, in extremes, it is not.

Unfortunately, burnout is a real thing. After observing this with other team members, I realized that I needed to become mindful and reflective of my feelings and ensuing behaviors, such as noticing myself having a shorter fuse or overwhelming feelings and exhaustion. This self-reflective practice has given me the awareness and tools to understand myself better, my motivations, and my behaviors. Additionally, I have found that having other team members who check in on each other has been essential to overall well-being. Everyone needs an outlet to share feelings and to debrief from tough cases. Checking in with fellow team members, recognizing the signs, and providing support can significantly help reduce team members' burnout. Being part of an interdisciplinary team provides this support.

I recently opened a private practice, reducing my regular connection with a multidisciplinary team. And I missed that connection. The solution came easily, and I joined a network of similar professionals and created a supervision group. Both types of connections provide an opportunity and safe space for other practitioners and me to check in on each other, debrief, and brainstorm. This is especially helpful with tough cases like Ron's and William's and to provide each other with emotional support when needed.

Reflective practice has allowed me to tune into my emotional state so that I know what I am taking into a client's room. Emotions are contagious, and clients can quickly become activated by your emotions, actions, and reactions, even when you think you have a poker face. If I rush in or I'm flustered, they sense it. If I'm tired or preoccupied, they sense it. My goal is to be the calm in their storm, not be a storm that blows into their room. This is particularly important when working with clients who have experienced traumatic events in their life. Unfortunately, given the statistics, it is highly likely that you have cared for clients who have experienced trauma and not even known it. As happened with William, behavior can easily be blamed on other things. Just as each of our clients' end-of-life experiences are unique, reactivation and triggers of traumatic experiences are unique.

Traumatic behavior responses can be triggered visually by touch, smells, certain words, or how you move toward someone. I think back to many clients who had distressing behaviors while their personal hygiene was being tended to. Knowing what I know now about trauma, I realize those behaviors could have been trauma-related responses to historical sexual assault. Furthermore, their "spidey senses" are often stuck on high alert, looking for danger and can be easily triggered. For example, I once had a client act out after being passed a drink. Using self-reflective practice, I considered my reactions. Was I being oversensitive—this behavior was from dementia—or could there be more to their story? I now take a moment before entering a client's space to check in with my emotions, take a deep breath, and ensure I'm grounded and fully present. Being aware of what I bring into the client's space reduces the chances of responsive behaviors, especially for those at end-of-life who may not be able to speak up for themselves.

The common thread in all these cases is the need for compassion. Clients do not choose to be difficult. People are complex, and adding the intricacies of end-of-life can create a perfect storm for perplexing behaviors. This reminds me of the story of Marjorie. Marjorie was a wonderful elderly woman who started shaking her hands in the last few months of her life. The hand movement reminded me of someone shaking and tossing dice.

One of the favorite parts of my job is getting to know my clients and hearing their stories. I enjoy learning about all their life experiences—the good and the bad. At the beginning of our relationship, Marjorie shared many stories of her small flock of chickens that she fed by hand daily. She loved her chickens. They gave her much joy, and she often sat outside on her porch watching them. Remembering this, her behavior made perfect sense. She was feeding her beloved birds. Knowing Marjorie more personally gave me knowledge and details I could use to help alleviate suffering. When she became anxious and unsettled, I found playing nature sounds with bird calls would help calm and soothe her.

Interestingly, in her final days, she insisted that we help get all the chickens back into the chicken coop. People often give cues that they are ready to die, such as packing a suitcase or sometimes seeing deceased loved ones who have come to meet them. After Marjorie's death, her daughter reflected on that moment. She wondered if her mother, trying to get the chickens back into the coop, symbolized her mother trying to put everything in order before she died. While we agreed it was possible, only Marjorie knows for sure.

End-of-life is one of the most intimate, hallowed experiences I have ever had the privilege of witnessing. I am humbled and honored to walk alongside someone as they navigate life's most intimate moments. Showing compassion, suspending judgment, listening to clients' life stories, and being curious about a client's behavior has allowed me to build deeper connections and rapport, creating a brave space for people to share and explore their thoughts and feelings.

I also try to remember to apply that same compassion to myself. Understanding my own emotions and behaviors, especially when they become overwhelming. This is crucial for my client's well-being and my own. I regularly see a therapist to explore any thoughts, emotions, or unusual behaviors of my own that I have noticed bubbling up to the surface.

My wish for everyone is to be curious daily about behavior: your own, the people around you, and always your clients. After all, someday, we will be at the end of our lives, likely being cared for by family and an end-of-life team. I can only hope that my end-of-life care team knows that *all behavior has meaning*.

৪০ ৫৪

Self-Care Tip

I have found that self-care has become an important buzzword over the past few years, especially for caregivers. For me, self-care includes eating well, hiking with my dog, connecting with friends, and even getting a good night's sleep. I feel that self-care is not just one thing like a bubble bath or meditation but a mix of things interwoven into day-to-day life. All of these things help me stay happy and healthy and able to better serve my clients.

Tip or Strategy for Other Practitioners and Caregivers

Through my years of working with clients, I have discovered the importance of knowing my own triggers and limits when it comes to what I can do when working with someone navigating end-of-life. By knowing my boundaries, I can better assist the ones I can and refer those I cannot work with to other practitioners. In addition, it keeps me mentally healthy and allows clients to have the best care possible.

Something I Wish I Had Known When I Started

After experiencing several personal losses in my life, I entered this profession to help others help people navigate their end-of-life journeys better than I had experienced with my loved ones. I thought I could help fix the system, but I quickly learned that although I could advocate for change, it is not my job to fix clients. It is my role to walk alongside them. It's kind of like being a "tour guide" along their life path.

ഽ ଔ

> "Bearing witness to the struggles of others;
> it is not about judging or directing these struggles."
> ~ Dr. Wolfelt, *Companioning the Bereaved*

The understanding of bearing witness to someone's struggles, especially after being diagnosed with a terminal illness, has dramatically changed throughout my lifetime. Initially, I thought of it as a passive role and was not an active participant. Sitting vigil at the bedside of someone dying, I was essentially sitting on the sidelines and watching as the client went through the phases of dying. However, the more I experienced death and dying, the more I realized how complex death is. I quickly learned that death is romanticized on television and in movies, that one does not just close their eyes and fall into what looks like a deep sleep with all their loved ones around their bedside. Death is messy and complicated, with people experiencing physical and emotional struggles. I sometimes found it overwhelming and wanted to jump in with both feet to help ease their suffering.

I got into this profession after experiencing many tragic losses in my own life and wanted to help others as they navigate their end-of-life journey. I wanted to help. I wanted to fix all the things I had seen go terribly wrong in the past, make things better, and ease suffering for those at the end of their life. However, I learned that while I can help with comfort measures such as advocating for better pain management, I cannot remove all of their sufferings. I realized there is profound truth in bearing witness to someone's struggles at the end of life. First, it is a very active role, not necessarily physically but in the emotional support of holding space and walking alongside clients as they navigate end-of-life struggles. My job is to bear witness, be non-judgmental and compassionate, and turn towards their suffering and walk with them instead of trying to fix it.

Second, I recognize that bearing witness to others' suffering as they navigate end-of-life challenges me to reflect on my own death. By holding space and turning towards their suffering, I also help myself reflect on the suffering I may experience with my own death. I, too, am going to die. I, too, am going to struggle. The supportive end-of-life team surrounding me will not be able to fix all my suffering at the end of my life. There will be some struggles and emotional suffering which I must journey through on my own. Therefore, I feel it is essential to do the emotional work now, to explore what death and dying means to me so that when it comes time for my own death, I can leave this world in a gentler way.

Book Recommended by Patti Broadfoot

Being Mortal:
Medicine and What Matters in the End
~ Atul Gawande

Dr. Atul Gawande's book challenged and inspired me to become a practitioner who looks at a client holistically and comprehensively. Dr. Gawande challenges Western healthcare thinking about saving someone's life at any cost and, more importantly, how these life-saving measures may significantly reduce the quality of life in the last months and days. I learned the importance of having hard conversations about what quality of life means to clients instead of what I believe will help them as they navigate serious illnesses or the end-of-life process. Having a better quality of life to the very end has now become one of my top priorities when caring for someone navigating end-of-life.

About the Book

Medicine has triumphed in modern times, transforming the dangers of childbirth, injury, and disease from harrowing to manageable. But when it comes to the inescapable realities of aging and death, what medicine can do often runs counter to what it should.

Through eye-opening research and gripping stories of his own patients and family, Gawande reveals the suffering this dynamic has produced. Nursing homes, devoted above all to safety, battle with residents over the food they are allowed to eat and the choices they are allowed to make. Doctors, uncomfortable discussing patients' anxieties about death, fall back on false hopes and treatments that are actually shortening lives instead of improving them.

In his bestselling books, Atul Gawande, a practicing surgeon, has fearlessly revealed the struggles of his profession. Now he examines its ultimate limitations and failures- in his own practices as well as others' — as life draws to a close. Riveting, honest, and humane, *Being Mortal* shows how the ultimate goal is not a good death but a good life — all the way to the very end.

Patti Broadfoot, RSW

Patti is an end-of-life social worker, grief counselor, and educator registered with the Ontario College of Social Workers and Social Service Workers. She is also a member of the Ontario and Canadian Association of Social Workers, Bereavement Ontario Network, and the Death Doula Ontario Network. Patti has over twenty-five years of experience working with a diverse clientele of children, adolescents, and adults in healthcare and education. Her area of expertise is in complicated, traumatic death and non-death losses.

Contact Information:
Phone: 226-270-5028
Email: info@innersojourn.net
Website: www.innersojourn.net

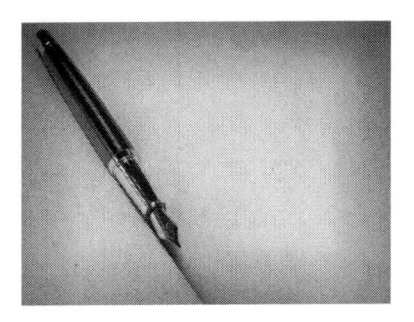

Reflection Questions for the Reader

What did you like best about this chapter?

_____
_____
_____
_____
_____
_____

What was your favorite passage in this chapter? Why did it stand out?

_____
_____
_____
_____
_____
_____

What feelings did this chapter evoke for you?

_____

_____

_____

_____

_____

If you had the chance to ask the author a question, what would it be?

_____

_____

_____

_____

_____

What form of action does this chapter inspire you to take?

_____

_____

_____

_____

_____

What did you know about this chapter's content before you read it?

_____
_____
_____
_____
_____
_____

What new things did you learn from reading this chapter?

_____
_____
_____
_____
_____
_____

What questions do you still have?

_____
_____
_____
_____
_____
_____

What else have you read on this topic?

_____

_____

_____

_____

_____

_____

Please visit **TenderTruthsCaringForTheDying.com** for more information, including the opportunity to meet the author during an online author and reader gathering.

CHAPTER 2

HONORING SACRED TRUTHS OF LIVING AND DYING WHILE INDIGENOUS
Chrystal Waban

"Have courage. You are not alone."

~ Author Unknown

Indigenous people are chronically at risk of premature death. This knowledge is historical and generational and saturates every aspect of life and awareness for each new generation. There are many ways that Indigenous people work to reduce the likelihood of premature deaths, such as suicide, overdose, violence, and crime.

In Canada, we have numerous days which raise awareness:

May 5th, *National Day of Awareness for Missing and Murdered Indigenous Women and Girls and Two-Spirit People* (MMIWG2S),

September 30th, *Orange Shirt Day*, Canada's first National Day for Truth and Reconciliation, to honor the survivors and victims of the residential school system and reflect on the atrocities Canada committed against Indigenous Peoples, including measures to successfully "kill the Indian in the child," and

October 4th, *Sisters in Spirit Day*, honoring missing and murdered Indigenous women and girls who are no longer walking this earth with us and showing support for their loved ones.

Perhaps this reality predestined me to be a death worker. It wasn't until I was several years into my healing journey that I began to find myself moving toward end-of-life care. As an Anishinaabekwe or Algonquin woman with mixed European ancestry, this is saying a lot.

I have been through more hard times and experiences than good. Chronic homelessness, mental illness, disability, poverty, violence, and trauma are aspects of my life cycle and that of my family, adding to lived expertise of my teaching bundle. These are not claims that I make easily, but it is my truth and my story that I am here to share.

Perhaps what has made writing this chapter so difficult is that I am still living a tender truth.

There was a time when grief-filled spaces in my head were occupied solely with hurts from my past and present realities. As a child and later a youth, there were times that I struggled with bullying and trauma. I felt exhausted from the daily battle that was my life. Without an end in sight, this exhaustion led me to consider suicide, and only my sense of obligation to my younger siblings kept me tethered and out of reach from the reprieve I imagined would come from ending my life.

As a young, sole parent, I continued to struggle. I struggled with the grief and loss that stemmed from missing out on typical firsts for people my age: learning to drive, attending college, and buying a home. As a mom barely out of her teens, I knew there was more I should give my children. The loss of these experiences compounded and seemed to factor into what it was I should have had to give. Once again, I measured what I did not have and what I did-tethered only by the love

I had for my children and fear of the unknown that would be waiting for them in child welfare.

Those days are long behind me. The memories live under my surface; the pain of doing without was once quick to the forefront. I got my driver's license at twenty-eight, graduated from university at thirty-five, and finally moved into my forever home at thirty-seven. Some days I must consciously work to remember that I am more than my perceived deficits.

As a First Nations woman, this healing work has looked like recovering and reclaiming resilience and identity that I hadn't been raised with. The story of my great-grandparents' survivorship of Canada's residential school legacy courses through my blood, my cells, and onward to my children. Canada's history is known as the Residential and Day School Legacies, while in the US, it is known as the Indian Boarding School Legacy.

I am without the language my grandfather once spoke fluently and mourned the connections to Anishinaabemowin and the land taken away in one generation. I have wept for the disturbance, the hardness, and the mental illness that gripped the parenting styles of subsequent generations. The teaching that "I am everything my Ancestors prayed for" is tempered by ongoing work to remember that I am more than a culmination of my past experiences.

A tender truth about caring for the dying is that unaddressed grief for the lost relationships with those still living and out of reach can cause insurmountable pain. The history that Indigenous people carry in their DNA means that so many of us are silently battling against an early death as a direct result of the pain we carry from our own lives and the generations before us.

In 2014, I was struggling through my sociology degree, parenting my children, and struggling to keep our heads above water. At times I would work eighty hours over the course of four days to make ends meet by taking shifts at the Violence Against Indigenous Women's

Shelter, where I worked. Before long, I was utterly burnt out, and my life ground to a halt. Defeated and hollow, I knew my children were suffering most of all, and the feeling that I was failing them has always been the catalyst for my ability to walk through fire. This time felt different, and I could not shake off the stress I carried. I found myself once again fantasizing about the reprieve I imagined death would bring.

Paralyzed by physical pain, I stopped working for three weeks and took time to reflect while laid up in bed, unable to move without the help of my children, who were growing up too fast out of necessity. I knew something had broken in me, and I found a way to choose life. I got in to see my incredible family doctor, into counseling, and armed with a Complex Post-Traumatic Stress Disorder diagnosis, embarked on a medication journey. I cannot express how difficult it was to knowingly lean into the poverty with which I had grown familiar and uncomfortable. I thrashed against this poverty of failing my children to pursue my degree.

This time of healing opened my eyes in ways that I could never have anticipated.

The weeks of hustling to make ends meet and the school demands of my schedule had led me to put major demands of support and childcare upon my extended family. Without a co-parent to tag in, my siblings and parents were the only people I could impose upon to watch my kids. And they were fed up.

My children felt unwelcome and were often treated with frustration, leading them to beg not to be forced into the homes of their relatives. At the same time, both of my children were struggling with monumental challenges to their mental well-being and self-confidence, with safety at school, in my parents' home, or in the care of my siblings. My family was exasperated by my constant requests for help and the sad state of my finances. They were not better off and did what they could.

I feared losing my kids to the same fantasies of death as a reprieve I had had while growing up. I constantly feared losing them to child welfare since getting pregnant at eighteen. This constant fear is a generational reality of parenting while Indigenous. Child welfare outcomes pose unique risks to our lives. One only has to learn about Tina Fontaine's legacy as a ward of child welfare to understand this very real threat and fear.

That summer, I allowed myself to acknowledge how much my children were going through. I started identifying old patterns from the perspective of well-being and safety as my new and firm priority. I started to question moments when my children should have felt loved and happy, realizing for the first time how the opposite had been normalized for me over a lifetime.

From the beginning of my post-secondary journey, I experienced negativity where I should have felt encouragement. Time after time, my family and closest friends attempted to convince me to drop out, to quit whenever I came up against any obstacle. When I sought out their guidance or a shoulder to cry on, I heard speeches about how I was clearly destined to fail.

I was excited and attempted conversations about new learnings and the perspectives I was developing by engaging with those in my chosen field. Bursting with passion and excitement, I was motivated by the alignment with my way of looking at the world and the study of sociology. Discussions and readings of classic social theories made me giddy. What I had always considered an ability to see the big picture transformed into the knowledge that I was a sociologist.

My friends and family had no interest, tuned out, and gave me attitude and snide remarks. I made excuses for their lack of interest and kindness: They had other things on their mind. I was a weirdo and overly excited. It wasn't on them to return my enthusiasm. I was coming off as a know-it-all. I deserved comments that made me think badly about myself. They were looking out for me and loved me, so I must work to respect their opinions and integrate it into my way of knowing.

Eventually, I ran out of rationalizations. I came to understand that the people I loved and cared for were more interested and engaged in my losses and failures than they were in my wins. With open eyes, I began to understand that they only ever seemed positive or kind when I was fulfilling my obligations to meet their needs, solve their problems, or remain focused on their lives. Any mention of a problem I was facing garnered comments that I had done something to bring this upon myself through my own irresponsibility and should be ashamed. I was not deserving of the same consideration and care they expected from me.

What began to take a toll on my relationships was my healing journey. What began to cost me my connections was a sense of self-worth. My insistence on mutual respect truly threatened my relationships with extended family. I respected myself now. I valued myself now. There was no turning back once this change occurred. This transformation added miles to the chasm of distance between us, and suddenly, I began to understand why I had felt death was my only option while growing up.

I stayed awake at night thinking about their futures and outcomes without my involvement and care. It was difficult to make this realization about my parents, and one conversation with my sister stood out.

"What's going to happen when they die?" I asked her. "It's not like they have arrangements. Will they be cremated? Buried? How much will their funerals cost? Will we have to pay for it, or do they have anything set aside?"

"You're probably worrying about it more than they are," she countered.

And she was right. It has been over ten years since that conversation, and neither of my parents has ever broached anything about their end-of-life plans or wishes. They think and function completely differently from me and get through each day, one at a time.

These small realizations continued to stack up. Understanding that these family members simply did not reciprocate their concern for my well-being, in the same way, was essential to my growth. By understanding this and more about the people tasked with nurturing my ability to thrive in life, I finally began to get my priorities straight. I finally stopped behaving in a way that fueled my side of the co-dependencies I had been raised with.

The first step seemed most painful when I ended a friendship that had spanned twenty years. Watching our daughters play as they had since birth and seeing how terribly my daughter was treated snapped me out of my delusion. All at once, I came to understand how my unhealthy and imbalanced grasp of relationships had impacted my children, and I continued to find myself in emotional states where I did not want to live.

Unpacking how I had grown up with this maltreatment normalized took a lot of work. Always self-reflective and critical, it seemed easier to understand how to take responsibility for the unhealthy behaviors I had exhibited as a parent, a sibling, and a friend and took steps to address behaviors I continued to perpetuate. Eventually, I came to understand trauma bonding and learned to practice true and real accountability as a result.

I grieve that my family never got to know me. They learned how I survived and what I had to do to get by. They understood my soft spot for my siblings and nephews and how I had been conditioned to look out for them. This knowledge was easily weaponized against me.

In baby steps, I began to address the grief caused by rejecting what had been normalized in my upbringing. I set boundaries for the first time and suffered for years more, thinking I could identify some way to honor my needs and keep them close by. One wrong move would mean my children and I were banished from social and family gatherings. One negatively perceived boundary meant spending Christmas alone. One wrong boundary was reinforced, and I lost out on a full year of a loved one's life. This was particularly hurtful when my young nephews couldn't remember me once the water seemed to flow under the bridge. As time marched on, I came to understand that my family didn't see or value the compromises I was making. I was there to play a supportive role in their lives and nothing more.

Through counseling, I developed an understanding of how I was raised. I came to recognize my conditioned response to my family and friends, to fulfill a maternal role and expectation of nurturing and rescuing. This care should have come from healthy adults with positive parenting skills. The Residential School Legacy ensured that healthy parenting was not a part of my upbringing. The colonization of this country known as Canada helped to dismantle my family's wellness, one generation at a time, long before I became a parent.

Today, I don't fault anyone for these realities because, in their own ways, they were focused on their survival and their stories, truly doing the best that they could.

I had to decide what was best for my children; they were the only ones who were entitled to my nurturing and parenting energy. They had suffered long enough from my split focus and experienced enough negative role modeling. My counselor empowered me to arrive at the understanding that I still had time to show them that self-respect and autonomy mattered. I could role model something new. I could show them a person who did not fantasize about a reprieve found only in death. I could show them a person who loves life.

My own story and memories feel sad and pitiful when spoken aloud. I don't fault my memories and know they are all true. I don't fault myself for the choices I made for my family before I became a mother. And I don't fault myself for the choices I made after I became a mother.

With boundaries securely in place, I began to look around for connections that better fit the person I was trying to become. What I found surprised me.

Perhaps because of the residential schools or different cycles of learned behavior, I found extended family members who had been struggling along for years, just like me—an uncle here, a cousin there, and another cousin over there. Each one of them made me realize that what I had been going through was not isolated. They had been through their own experiences with suicidal ideation as well and knew how difficult it was to choose to live instead.

They were the family members who had been bad-mouthed endlessly, with hurtful gossip and untruths thrown about without care or concern. Each of us experienced amplified mistreatment and was disposed of when we didn't do exactly as prescribed by those who thought they knew us best. We were a small army of the walking wounded, and connecting with each one of them gave me the strength I needed to carry on. They are caring, wonderful people who I am grateful managed to survive their own dances with premature death.

Learning about and deciding on low contact or no contact relationships with loved ones became the most important decision for my own mental well-being. While it does get easier with time, it still makes me sad. It is sad and frustrating that people I love are incapable of being happy for me. It is sad that people I love are out of reach.

As my parents age and this death doula role grows within me, I imagine what it will feel like when they die. The chasm remains. Each time I see my parents and am confronted with their proximity to death, I find myself shaken and brought to tears at the reality. They appear smaller and less steady. I know they are both dying, and nothing I can do will make that a gentle process for them. As aunts and uncles depart this Earth, I know their time is coming, and I find myself trying to plan a way to cope with their deaths. No matter how sad I feel, my spiritual and cultural practice includes honoring the spectrum of life to value our end as much as our beginning. And all the hard stuff in between.

No matter how badly I wish I could care for them, my help is not welcome. No matter how deeply I love my parents, they will not reciprocate and behave like parents, and there's nothing I can do to change that.

In the beginning, I struggled immensely with reverting to what I always did: Apologizing for the sake of family connections and inclusion.

I still have immense love for people I don't speak to, and I often worry about their present realities and futures. I probably always will. I spent the first thirty years of my life feeling suicidal and struggling with chronic depression, and I couldn't seem to feel happy unless those I cared for were happy too.

The tender truth about dying for Indigenous people is that we are often fighting against our own premature death. The years I have spent working to learn and understand grief, death, and end-of-life have inspired much reflection. By fighting against feelings of worthlessness and doing without, I have managed to overcome my personal and imminent death by suicide. I am better off now that I have developed muscles of happiness from within. Resources help, and so does unlearning internalized racism. Wisdom is the sweetness of age.

To finally have healthy relationships, coping skills, and unconditional support in place has been everything. I thank my kids, husband, uncle, and cousins for holding space and indirectly offering validations to the choices I have struggled to make and keep. Each year that passes with my boundaries intact are years that my mental health and outlook on life improves. With these positive people around me, I can finally be the person I was meant to be.

As a death doula, these relationships consisting of grief and loss are plentiful in the lives of the people I support. Pain derived from abuse, rejection, and separation are equal to an actual end to someone's life. Sometimes we must grieve the loss of someone's presence in our lives long before they are gone from this earth. When the person we have grieved actually dies, we can be left with feelings of numbness or no feelings at all. It is rarely the family scenarios we see represented in media, which is a truth about dying that we rarely discuss.

There are many ways that Indigenous people are fighting against the premature deaths of themselves, their families, and community members. These folks are all death workers, striving to reduce harm and the likelihood of losing another soul to the history of genocide in North America. I am grateful to my Ancestors, who watch over me and guide me on this journey. Without them, I would have succumbed long ago.

॰ঃ ৫৯

Self-Care Tip

The self-care practice that has aided me in this work is debriefing with other practitioners. I am fortunate to be a member of the Indigenous Death Doula Collective, and this self-care is built into our relationships with each other. One only has to share that an experience or client session was heavy, and one after the other, offers to debrief pour in. Surrounding oneself with your peers can make all the difference.

Tip or Strategy for Other Practitioners or Caregivers

A time may come when you are caring for someone at end-of-life, and they may have a story of disenfranchised grief, like that, shared in my story. It may be less severe or worse. It is important to consider your capacity to support this individual appropriately. Evaluate and reflect on this capacity with honesty and if you feel lacking, consider reaching out to a practitioner specializing in complicated grief, loss, and end-of-life care.

A client may arrive in your practice who has been cut off and labeled unhealthy by family members, and the person dying tasks you with reaching out to see if they want to attend the relative's bedside, make amends, or say goodbye. This is also something that must be reflected upon before agreeing to provide care and support services.

It is better to make a referral than to cause harm, indirectly or otherwise. Each situation is unique and can only be addressed with a customized approach. It's okay and ethical to say no if these are not areas or situations you feel capable or comfortable navigating.

Something I Wish I Had Known When I Began on This Journey as a Practitioner in End-of-Life Care and What I Discovered About It

When I first began learning about disenfranchised and displaced grief, there was much more available to learn from than I had realized. People who are members of the LGBTQ community have been navigating this form of loss for ions, and many of the most helpful readings I found and participants of nurturing conversations I had came from this community. Chii Miigwetch (big thank you).

෴

> **"Going to the wilderness of the soul with another human being; it is not about thinking you are responsible for finding the way out."**
> ~ Dr. Wolfelt, *Companioning the Bereaved*

Honoring the spirit is reassurance, permission, and validation. I have felt called to give a dying person permission to let go, providing assurance that someone will look out for their loved ones and letting them know that their departure will not ruin the family. It might temporarily fell them, but it's not permanent. It is natural, and it is a part of life.

I'm thinking of my father-in-law, who died of early-onset dementia. He was nonverbal at the end. And I felt a real need when I was alone with him to let him know that his wife and sons would be okay and that he could let go of the responsibilities he felt toward them. By this time, they had spent so much time caring for him, and he was no longer the man they had known all their lives. I found myself speaking to him and giving him that permission he needed. He had never met me before having dementia, so he didn't have a connection with me. In a way, it was very much like supporting a client. I told him, "Don't worry. I will take care of them. I will be here for them, and we will celebrate you. You have to finish your journey." It's strange because in life, like in death, sometimes we need permission.

℘ ☙

> **"Discovering the gifts of sacred silence;**
> **it is not about filling up every moment with words."**
> ~ Dr. Wolfelt, *Companioning the Bereaved*

It's hard to get comfortable in silence. It can be hard if you're not comfortable and you don't have practice letting the silence be and serve its purpose that it's come to serve. It can be challenging for someone, and especially if you're new to this kind of work, you might have some nervous things about yourself. You might giggle if you're nervous, or you might chatter. It goes hand in hand with mindfulness, where when you're caring for that dying person, they might be in and out of consciousness. You might be ushering people in and out of the room or doing other things. And your role is to facilitate the silence. So it's not easy, and it takes practice, but it's something you can get practice doing. It is something you can increase your skills around. If you find it challenging, it might be a good idea to strategize and troubleshoot before you're in that situation. Learn to work with silence.

Silence is a mindfulness practice. You could go to a church and sit in silence. You could go to a river and sit in silence. Those are all really practical ways to start to find a comfort level with silence. You could set a regular timer on your phone to remind you to practice sitting in silence for five minutes. You could find opportunities to practice silence around other people. Yoga class will help you practice sitting in silence.

There are different versions of silence. There are ways for people to develop this comfort level. It does help to have busy work. For Indigenous people, it's super common to have handy crafts or lap tasks. You might be beading, or you could be sewing something; you might be making something. And specifically, when you're working with the dying, it's really common to create clothing and attire that they will wear on that final journey, something that you'll dress them in after they've gone. So, making moccasins and beading is common. You sit in silence, beading clothing, and different things. And now shrouds are becoming increasingly popular. So, the task may be creating that shroud. Some people are sewing them. Some are knitting them. If you really are struggling, that's one way to sit in silence. But it can also be part of the care you're giving. It's part of the ritual of the moment.

Dr. Wolfelt talks about "sacred silence," not just "silence." What comes to mind is it's a very important time of transition for that person, for that spirit, for that being. It's similar to birth, where sometimes it's not a silent thing at all. It can be quite loud. And if you're in a hospital setting, they'll tell you to quiet down so you don't scare the other people. Death is the opposite of that spectrum in all those ways. And with that transition from earthside to Sky World, that sacred silence, it's a time where you're calling in your Ancestors to receive that person. You're thinking about the people who've gone before them. You're thinking about the life they've lived. And it's a time of reflection and prayer and sacred communication with that spiritual kind of realm

One of our Creation Stories that we have is about the Midewiwin lodges. It talks about a rattle. I encourage our death doulas to have one of these rattles. To make one is a whole process. It also starts with the death of the animal offering itself to make the rattle. So, this rattle is part of the whole animal. The teeth from the animal make the rattle noise. It's a sacred object. Everything is silent, and a sacred fire is burning nearby, and that rattle is used to call in the Ancestors to help guide that person's soul on the journey back. It is silent, but it has instruments, for lack of a better word. There is a lot of mindfulness in the moment. But you're actively supporting a transition with your silence, and you don't speak words, but you make this rattling noise because only the ancestors can hear it.

Book Recommended by Chrystal Waban

Becoming Medicine:
Pathways of Initiation into a Living Spirituality
~ David R. Kopacz, MD & Joseph Rael

So many individuals are seeking something when navigating life, death, and everything in between. I found some answers about myself in this book and Joseph Rael's thoughts and affirmations about becoming medicine.

Some of us death workers feel a calling to this work, and I am no different. This book helped me to understand my role in creating healing spaces while unlocking self-imposed obstacles when developing my practice as a helper.

About the Book

In a time when many are feeling lost, this second collaboration by holistic psychiatrist David Kopacz and Native American visionary Joseph Rael offers hope. Becoming Medicine takes us on a journey into the heart of the medicine wheel where separation and division are replaced by an experience of spiritual democracy and unity with all people, with nature, and with the cosmos. Following the ancient pathways of initiation of mystics, visionaries, and shamans we learn everyone can find a living spirituality-a connection to the source of all religions. Learning from mystics and visionaries such as Jung, Corbin, Rumi, Whitman, Alice & John Coltrane, and Miles Davis, the book brings together threads of ancient and modern wisdom paths. When we make the secret journey into the heart at the center of the medicine wheel, we are becoming medicine, becoming the healing that our world so desperately needs today.

Chrystal Waban Toop, RSSW

Chrystal is a circle keeper, public speaker, Doula, Counselor, and Registered Social Services Worker. Through her mixed Omamiwinini ancestry, Chrystal has reclaimed connections with her traditional community, Pikwakanagan First Nation. Her heartwork as the Founder of Blackbird Medicines, a grassroots movement that advances healing justice through support from urban and rural First Nations collaborators. Together, they offer several community-led projects, including the Indigenous Death Doula Collective and Endayan Mashkiikii (My Home Medicines).

Contact Information:
Email: **blackbirdmedicines@gmail.com**
Website: www.blackbirdmedicines.ca and www.ogimakwe.com

Reflection Questions for the Reader

What did you like best about this chapter?

_____

_____

_____

_____

_____

_____

What was your favorite passage in this chapter? Why did it stand out?

_____

_____

_____

_____

_____

_____

What feelings did this chapter evoke for you?

If you had the chance to ask the author a question, what would it be?

What form of action does this chapter inspire you to take?

What did you know about this chapter's content before you read it?

What new things did you learn from reading this chapter?

What questions do you still have?

What else have you read on this topic?

_____

_____

_____

_____

_____

_____

Please visit www.TenderTruthsCaringForTheDying.com for more information, including the opportunity to meet the author during an online author and reader gathering.

CHAPTER 3

IS IT POSSIBLE TO PRAY THE WRONG PRAYER?
Rusty Williams

> "When you were born, you cried and the world rejoiced. Live your life so that when you die, the world cries and you rejoice."
>
> ~ Cherokee Proverb

Five minutes before pulling that chair up to the side of her bed, I had been patrolling the streets and neighborhoods in my assigned sector of a town of roughly forty-two square miles with just over 23,000 residents. It was about a week before Christmas, just after eleven at night, and my shift would be over in an hour. I was dispatched to an unconscious person at a house in my sector. The dispatcher gave no further information other than Emergency Medical Services (EMS) had been dispatched.

The dispatcher informed me that the caller only said, "She's unconscious, hurry!" before hanging up. In the couple of minutes it took me to get to that home, with lights flashing and siren blazing, I couldn't help but wonder what the cause of the state of unconsciousness was. To help prepare you to do your best when arriving at the scene, medical and police training condition you to anticipate the worst. The worst *physical* condition that is.

And, when that training kicks in—Bam! Bam! Bam!—muscle memory and prior experience take over, giving the victim the best possible outcome. But, when I got up to that bedroom, I discovered that the victim did not want the best possible outcome. She wanted to die peacefully. And that was in direct opposition to the wishes of her family.

Everything was on autopilot until I got to her bedroom: I had parked my patrol car away from the driveway so the ambulance could get in, I had all the medical equipment I carried in the trunk of my car, and I used my "Where is she so I can help her?" voice in a direct but respectful way. It wasn't until I saw who I was called to take care of that I realized this wasn't anything I had been trained for.

Is it possible to pray the wrong prayer? That's what I was thinking as I pulled a chair up to the side of her bed. I had been a cop for over three years and spent the four-and-half years before that serving as a paramedic in a city that was the poorest and the most violent in the United States at that time. So, the prior seven years had prepared me for just about any emergency. In my role as a paramedic, I was an instructor in Advanced Cardiac Life Support; even though it had been more than three years since I was responsible for the care of those who were sick, I was still confident in my skillset.

A woman in her forties was lying in a bed in the master bedroom, surrounded by bottles and containers of all kinds of medicine. She looked frail, was jaundiced, and she looked at me when I got up to the side of the bed. I was expecting an unconscious person, and I found myself looking down at a conscious person. She was not only conscious and able to talk, not clearly or with much strength, but there was no doubt in her telling me, "I told them not to call you."

The man who had identified himself as her husband spoke up. He said he wanted me to do everything I could to save her. This man desperately didn't want his wife to die. He told me she had cancer, and it had spread. But he also said they had faith, and regardless of what the doctors told her, he knew she would be alright if they prayed.

I looked around the room, and it was obvious this was a family of the Catholic faith. There was a crucifix hanging above the bed and a statue of the Virgin Mary on the bureau. A set of rosary beads was on the nightstand among the different bottles of medication that had been prescribed to her. The husband interrupted what I was taking in by telling me to get working on her. He demanded that I give her oxygen. This woman didn't appear to be having major breathing problems, so I took a moment to regain my thoughts (all my training and experience had gone out the window by this point).

The woman, shaking her head "no" at her husband's insistence on oxygen, motioned for me to bend over to hear her. She spoke slowly and softly, but what she told me was clear. She said her cancer had spread throughout her body and her doctor told her the best he could do was prescribe medication to make her comfortable. The doctor suggested she would be more comfortable in the hospital, but she wanted to die in her home. She then told me she had a living will (this was back in the late 1980s before they were called advanced directives, and her Living Will included an explicit Do Not Resuscitate (DNR) clause).

Her husband had it in his hand when I turned to ask him where it was. As he handed it to me, he told me he didn't care what the will said; he had faith that God would keep her alive and cure her if everyone prayed hard enough.

That line, "If everyone prayed hard enough," hit me like a piece of lumber across my forehead. That was almost the exact phrase I told my dad and anyone else who would listen when my mom was told there was nothing the doctors could do for her after her breast cancer spread to her bones and eventually to her brain. That was three years earlier, and I was still hurting from the sting of her death. My mom died an hour after I finished my first shift as a police officer; my first day on the job as a cop ended with my mom's death. My dad died the following Thanksgiving morning from lung cancer that spread to his brain.

After my mom was diagnosed, I prayed and prayed hard (and often), trusting in the God I was told would do anything if asked in Jesus' name. However, it seemed the harder I prayed, the sicker my mom got. Hospice was in its infancy in the middle 1980s, and my mom was admitted into a nursing home to spend the remainder of her days. I got to her bed just in time to see her take her last breath.

My dad, who had been diagnosed with lung cancer shortly after my mom was diagnosed with breast cancer, died alone in a hospital room the following Thanksgiving morning. He died alone, found during a shift change around seven in the morning. I still remember the phone call that morning, asking if I was the son of Russell Williams, then being informed that he had died sometime during the night.

Between the time of my mom's death and my dad being told his cancer had spread, I decided I must have prayed the wrong prayer or prayed the wrong way that led to God not curing my mom. Admittedly, when you're in your early twenties and your theology is in its infancy stage as an adult, you tend to think differently than a sixty-one-year-old ordained minister. But I still thought I had God on my side when my dad's cancer spread, so I changed things up in my prayer routine. Surely, God would spare my dad's life so my brother and I wouldn't be orphans at an age where we were just old enough to legally drink beer!

Unfortunately, my new prayer routine didn't affect my dad's outcome. So, on that Thanksgiving morning when my dad died, I decided I didn't need this kind of god in my life and told God to . . . well, let's just say I had a few choice words for this so-called benevolent god. It's not that I stopped believing in God. I just decided to go it alone; who needs this kind of god—a god who ignores prayers—in their life?

All these thoughts and memories flooded my mind as I listened to this man who didn't want to lose his wife, the same way my dad didn't want to lose his wife just a few years earlier. And this couple had children—two girls. Both were in the home, and both were upset. One appeared to be in her early twenties, and the other looked like she was in her late teens. Their tears, worry, and words intensified my thoughts and memories. They were so close to my brother's age and my age when our mom died. Indeed, I thought to myself, *There was no training for this.*

My focus returned to where I was, and I looked closer at the living will the husband had handed me and saw the number for her doctor. I asked the husband if I could use their phone to call his wife's doctor (before the advent of cell phones). I called the number and left a message with his answering service. A few minutes later, the doctor called back. He confirmed that the woman, his patient, wanted to die at home, and he confirmed the DNR order.

I was now caught in the middle between this woman's legal rights, her wishes, and her family's wishes. And I was dealing with my own feelings and memories of my parents' deaths. As each moment passed, the husband became more aggressive and insisted that his wife be transported to the hospital. The more agitated the husband became, the more his wife tried to reassure him that she would be okay. I was in a place I had never been before and where I had received no training.

I did my best to explain to the husband that his wife had a right to be where she wanted to be, and that right was memorialized in a legal document and confirmed by her doctor. From a strictly legal and law enforcement operational stance, my services were no longer needed at this house. But, from a human place of understanding, I knew I had to stay and offer whatever talents God might give me on this night. So, I called my sergeant and explained the situation to him.

Our talk was part policy discussion and part being a decent human being discussion. The policy discussion was on the requirements of a police officer at an unattended death. If a qualified medical professional doesn't attend a death, the police must respond and complete certain checklists and ensure a crime wasn't committed, or at the very least, the death wasn't suspicious. If I left the home and later this woman died, an officer from the next shift would have to respond and treat it like a crime scene until a medical examiner either responded or was satisfied with the picture painted by the officer. On most occasions, a detective would respond and investigate the scene and make the call to the medical examiner. Department resources would be tied up for hours.

However, with a DNR in a living will, if a person died in the presence of a law enforcement officer, the death wasn't considered an unattended death, and a funeral director could be called immediately. In this case, if I stayed at the house, the family would be spared the questions that must be asked in an unattended death investigation, and the woman would be removed from the home in a more dignified way (by the funeral director instead of the medical examiner). Since I had already established rapport with the woman, I asked my sergeant if I could stay at the home until she died. I felt a need to be there; there's no better way to explain it than that.

My sergeant agreed, and I put all my medical equipment back in the patrol car and went back upstairs to the bedroom. But the husband said he didn't want to watch his wife die and told me to call down to him when that happened. He said he and his daughters would be downstairs praying.

Praying for what? I wondered.

I sat down again by her side, not knowing what to do or say. The woman had drifted off again, and she appeared to be in a state of unconsciousness. I didn't know how long it would be but judging from her breathing, I assumed it wouldn't be that long before she died.

Sitting there, in complete silence with her, my mind returned to the memories of my parents and their deaths. I thought about how hard I had prayed and imagined this woman's family had prayed just as hard for her. What went wrong with our prayers?

The woman opened her eyes and looked at me. She told me she knew her family feared her death. She explained how she tried to console them and explain herself and her feelings at other times. She then began asking me questions: Was I married? Did I have any children? How long was I a police officer?

I found it easy to answer her questions, and those answers led to discussions. At times, she drifted off, and her breathing became shallow. But after some time, she'd open her eyes and look around the room. I noticed how her eyes were sunken from the ravages cancer had taken on her body. We had more conversations, but each one was shorter than the one before, and the length of her unconscious state grew. Finally, after a few hours, she opened her eyes and asked for her rosary beads and for me to pray for her.

I handed her the beads that were on the night table by the bed and asked her what she wanted me to pray. She said she wanted me to pray for her to have a nice death. And she asked me to pray that it would come very soon. Her voice was now barely audible, and I had to lean down to her face to hear her. But her request was clear.

Since she closed her eyes after that request, I didn't feel the need to close mine when I began to pray. I simply said to myself, *Lord, help this woman die peacefully, and she's asked that it happen soon.* After repeating it in my mind, I thought about the prayers her husband and two daughters were saying downstairs. I knew their prayers were the opposite of what I was praying. There was a combat of prayers going on in that house: the husband's and daughters' versus mine.

And I couldn't help but imagine what God must have been processing as that was going on.

I can share with you that it was a privilege to witness this woman's transition from this life to the next (if you believe that happens when a person dies). She died within an hour of that last time she spoke to me, asking me to pray for her. And I'm also happy to share that her husband and daughters found the courage to come upstairs when I called them as her breathing was slowing considerably; they were there when she died.

I was weary driving home afterward. My shift was supposed to end at midnight, and I didn't get home until around four in the morning. On that drive home, I wondered if I had betrayed the husband and his two daughters with my prayer. I second-guessed whether I should have prayed with them for a miracle that night. And the question, *Did God really listen to me more than her husband and daughters?* kept playing over and over as I tossed and turned in bed for the rest of the night.

Between that night and tonight, the night I'm writing this part of this chapter, a lot of things have happened. First and foremost, I've matured as a person, which means my theology has matured. I've endured the loss of colleagues and friends and experienced the pain and grief of divorce. I was diagnosed with a tumor growing in my spinal cord thirteen years ago. Because of that, I've learned what it means to lose everything (my physical mobility and financial stability, including our home).

But through all that, I've grown and experienced more joy in life than I ever thought possible. I met, fell in love with, and married the love of my life; my two boys are now successful young men starting their own families; my professional CV now includes ordained minister as a job title.

The most important change—the most significant happening—in my personal life is I no longer see death as the enemy; I no longer feel it's important to defeat death at every step. Let me explain.

My first full-time job was a summer job as a lifeguard. Every summer when school was out, from when I was fifteen until I was eighteen, I worked as a lifeguard. That job's main function is to ensure swimmers don't die by drowning. The name itself, *lifeguard*, is an explicit description—guard life.

After gaining a nice tan for those four summers, it was time to get a real job. I became an Emergency Medical Technician (EMT) during my senior year in high school. I volunteered on our local emergency squad when the director for a new type of medical program in New Jersey suggested I apply. At nineteen, I was accepted into the New Jersey College of Medicine and Dentistry training program to become a paramedic. For the next four and half years, I worked as a paramedic in that poor and violent city I mentioned at the beginning of this chapter. Once again, as a lifeguard in high school, I fought against death. Only this time, I had medications and adjunctive equipment to assist me in that fight; surely, the advanced training I received and all the technology and skills I possessed would help in that fight against death.

Unfortunately, more people died than were saved during my tenure as a paramedic—exponentially, many more died than were saved. And many of those individuals were children. To this day, I wake up soaked in sweat, screaming (according to my wife) with the images of those children just as real as they were when I was working on them. I was burnt out and knew I had to find a different career. The town where I had volunteered as an EMT was hiring police officers. I was fortunate that during my time as an EMT, I developed relationships with most of the police officers.

After eleven years in the patrol division, I was reassigned to the detective bureau and spent the rest of my career there. As a detective, I learned how to process crime scenes and interview suspects. Some of those scenes and suspects had to do with death—either suspicious death or homicide. And, once again, death was a negative. It was such a negative that anyone who was found to be responsible for a death, based in part on my investigation, was sentenced to a long time in prison.

It wasn't until seminary that I learned that death isn't the enemy. It is a guarantee of life.

So, if it's a guarantee, why do we villainize it?

That question I had to come to grips with allowed me to finally grieve my parent's death more than twenty years after they were gone.

Once I came to grips with that, as if on cue, I remembered a conversation I had with the priest who officiated both my parents' funeral services. He told me that after my mom died, my dad was depressed. And after he learned that his cancer had returned and his condition worsened, he told this priest that he was looking forward to being reunited with his wife.

My dad wasn't afraid of death, and the healing he wanted was spiritual, not physical. And yet, not knowing that, I prayed as hard as I could that he would be cured. Once again, as with the prayers on that night spent with the woman who died, there were opposing prayers heading out to God (or the Universe, or whatever one believes is out there).

My dad died, and yet, paradoxically, he was healed. I denied that paradoxical truth until I accepted another truth: Death is not the enemy. I have to wonder how many of us accept this. How many of us understand that healing doesn't always mean physical healing. When I think back to that night in that bedroom with the dying woman, I now see the healing that took place. Yes, there was indeed healing that night.

She was healed from the worry she felt for her family as they gathered around her and said their goodbyes before taking her last breath. She was coherent enough to acknowledge each one of them. Her family experienced a special healing that night as well. They were healed from the anger at her for wanting to die peacefully at home, and the conflict that existed between their wishes (prayers?) and hers resulted in a loving healing as they all accepted her death.

Right now, if you're thinking, "If that's the case, what is healing, and how do I pray for it?" I promise that you're in good company. You're in good company not just with what we ordained folks call the laity, you're also in good company with those of us in the clergy as well. And, no matter what answer I offer—whatever pearls of wisdom I've been taught or have experienced—the truth is, I don't think there is a direct answer to that question. But, if you have one, I'd love to hear it!

When I look back at my life and the lives of people I've known, I see how so often the healing that took place was a healing that wasn't specifically asked for. And, since seminary and ordination, I've learned and experienced a lot about prayer. Both answered and unanswered. When prayers are answered, all seems right with the world, and we praise God for coming to the rescue. And, when our prayers aren't answered, we either get angry at God, or we make excuses for God and say things like, "It was her/his time," or "God must have needed an angel."

With prayer, we rarely reflect on the event in a way that leaves God out of the equation. For many people, a contract of sorts is created through prayer and the person's belief system or relationship with God. Before ordination, I participated in what some call *transactional theology*. Transactional theology is the belief that if I do something for God, God will do something in-kind for me; and, if God does something for me (an answered prayer), I must do something for God. In either case, a transaction takes place between the person and God.

I call this *vending machine theology,* where God is the vending machine, and the dollar bill we will insert in that slot is prayer. We put the dollar bill in the machine and expect the machine to drop our selected item to the tray at the bottom. A transaction occurred: The dollar bill went into the machine, and the item requested was delivered in return. That works well until we insert the dollar bill (pray), and either nothing falls to the bottom tray, or the wrong item is delivered (unanswered prayer).

When my parents died, I believed the problem was with me or the dollar itself (with my prayers). God was all-loving, so there couldn't be anything wrong with the machine (after all, an all-loving God wouldn't let my parents die and leave my brother and me orphans at such young ages). So, the only thing that could have been wrong was my prayers (the dollar bill) or that I was such a lousy person God didn't see fit to answer my prayers.

This is a trap for many people who feel unworthy of God's love or believe they aren't praying the right way. However, suppose we're willing to change our mindset about prayer to that of moving away from transactional theology to one of transformational faith. In that case, we'll begin to see the kind of healing that took place with my parents, with that family I've been talking about, and especially with ourselves.

It's important to remember that prayers for physical healing, whether answered or unanswered, are a way we connect with God. Whatever you perceive God to be, whatever your faith or beliefs, when we pray, we enter a very special connection with the Divine. And that special connection is both intimate and personal. So, maybe the best way to pray for healing is to pray for healing that only God knows the person being prayed for needs. Okay, maybe it's not the best way, but it's hard to argue it's not the safest way.

If we believe in an omniscient God, then we agree that God knows what's needed more than we do. So, yes, praying for healing in a generic way is a safe way to pray if we don't want to get angry or think something is wrong with us or our prayers. But it's also an honest way to simply hold someone special in our hearts and share that intimate relationship with God. No one would argue that praying a specific prayer is wrong. And, just as surely, no one would argue that a simple connection with God with a person's name (or image) is also wrong.

If we allow ourselves to think about these truths, we won't build a trap where we think we've prayed wrong when physical healing isn't the result. As a minister, I can't imagine a divine entity being upset with anyone who takes the time to connect on that very personal level. Instead, the fact that you took the time to lift someone in prayer would surely make the Divine smile.

As health declines in people we love and care about, it's only natural to want them to get better. Any prayers we've shared weren't wasted and certainly weren't in vain. Instead, they were a loving example of our love, compassion, empathy, and concern. Our prayers can become a loving example of our relationship with that person and an opportunity to consider our relationship with the Divine. Because when we pray, we can also use our hands and feet in addition to our hearts. And that can move us to spend time with those in need. It means we'll share our own vulnerability and fears by sitting quietly with someone who is dying—and nothing we can do will change that outcome. That knowledge alone can be scarier than hell, so we might also pray for strength for ourselves to spend whatever time is left with those we love with an open mind and a soft heart.

Maybe it's only after we've spent that time with a loved one that we'll look back and see that our prayer for strength was answered; after all, we sat with that person, listened to them, and shared stories. The strength we asked for did indeed manifest itself. And maybe that small win in our faith journey will allow us to see where our prayers—even though the person died—were indeed answered. The person we loved experienced a healing that is all but unexplainable.

You see, prayer can be so much more than words sent up an imaginary pipeline to heaven. Prayer can be, and often is, simply being present with someone who is suffering. Prayer is sharing love and opening up to the wholeness of life with another who might be dying. The late Episcopal Bishop John Spong once described prayer as entering into the pain or joy of another person, of what is being done when one loves wastefully and passionately and wondrously and invites others to do so.

With that in mind, is there any use in worrying if we've prayed the wrong way or if we need to change our prayer? When we enter into a relationship with someone who is dying, isn't that a very deep level of prayer? And if it is, do our words (or thoughts) sent up to Heaven matter more than our presence with that person?

When we become aware that death is imminent, we stop all the unnecessary game-playing that is so common in all relationships and instead become present in a beautiful form of prayer. Those of us in chaplaincy work call this *the ministry of presence*. Our simple, quiet presence is perhaps the most loving gift we can offer to the person dying and to their family and loved ones.

How often do our words close us off from the actual experience? When we share life intimately with someone dying, simply being there with them opens us up to an awareness of all that's around and within us. I would submit to you that this, too, is a beautiful form of prayer.

If we were to compare the rote words of prayer to the ministry of presence, sharing our company intimately in a painful situation, there's no question which is the most honest form of prayer. The power of that experience of our presence in the life of someone who knows they are dying is greater than all the clichés we use in prayer.

Instead of demanding that God comply with our desires in any given moment (pleading prayers of intercession), seeking a connection with the Divine in that ministry of presence is like a gift of love that is shared with reckless abandon. It's an example of what the late Bishop meant when he described prayer as loving wastefully, passionately, and wondrously and inviting others to do so.

Understanding now that prayer has many forms, instead of questioning ourselves if we've prayed the wrong prayer when physical healing doesn't happen, we can change our way of praying. Instead of words, we can move to a prayer of presence with the dying person, giving them the opportunity to share all they need or want to share with us.

When we do that, our most precious gift of prayer is making certain that the person with a terminal illness doesn't walk that journey alone. And, when that happens, so does healing.

℘ ☙

Self-Care Tip

The self-care tip I continue to work on is being gentle with myself. I often remind myself that I am human – we're all only human. Blaming myself and second-guessing my words and actions often leads to unhealthy emotions, and I find myself on autopilot with unproductive thought patterns. One of the ways I remind myself to remain gentle with myself is by imagining the pre-flight briefing whenever I travel by plane. That briefing tells everyone in the plane that, in the event of a loss of cabin pressure, we're to put on our own oxygen masks first before assisting others. That reminder brings me to an affirmation that has helped me help others: I am worthy and deserving of being the best version of myself.

Strategy to Help Other Practitioners and Caregivers

There will be times, if they haven't already happened, when you experience a conflict between what the patient wants and what their loved ones want. And while any medical-legal discussion is beyond the scope of this chapter (and book), the caregiver needs to understand the need to remain calm and impartial. And that includes keeping an impartial spiritual mindset, too. Our own beliefs, faith upbringing, religious practices, and social stances all influence our thoughts. When confronted with a situation where the wishes of others or our own beliefs and desires contradict those of the patient, we must understand the needs and wishes of the patient are paramount. Remaining impartial with an open mind (and an open heart) will allow us to step into that awareness of the presence of the Divine, no matter how or what we or anyone else is praying for.

Something I Wish I Had Known When I Began on This Journey as a Practitioner in End-of-Life Care and What I Discovered About It

I wish I knew the importance of self-forgiveness and being gentle with myself. Regarding ministering (chaplaincy work), I moved past being hard on myself (beating myself up) for not knowing what to say or do and holding myself accountable for every failure of my past (non-forgiving of myself) for not living up to my own standards. And in doing so, I became a better chaplain, and I'm now better equipped to minister to those who are dying and grieving.

ഔ ൙

> **"Respecting disorder and confusion; it is not about imposing order and logic."**
> ~ Dr. Wolfelt, *Companioning the Bereaved*

The tender truth is as simple as honoring the person's journey. It's a natural desire (and need) for people to have reason and organization in their lives. So, when we're with someone whose life has been turned upside down, we find ourselves in an uncomfortable situation. We want and need order and logic, and the person we are with is amid disorder and confusion.

The last thing a dying person needs is someone trying to enforce reason and organization into their life; what they need is for us to allow them to simply be themselves. Reminding them that whatever feelings or emotions they are experiencing are normal encourages them to be where they are. Instead of trying to fix the chaos in their life, by respecting the disorder and confusion they are experiencing, we can offer them the loving gift of accepting them for who and where they are.

Most of us have a desire to help fix a problem when we encounter it; I know when I was a paramedic in my early twenties and especially during my twenty-five-year police career, my job required that I try to fix whatever was wrong. Since becoming an ordained minister, I've learned the importance of meeting people where they are – even if that means being uncomfortable. By meeting the other person where they are, we demonstrate that the encounter is not about us; our time together is about them – it's about their wishes, stories, and needs.

One of the most honest ways we can acknowledge death is to accept the disorder and confusion surrounding it. Even in the most peaceful of hospice settings, death often brings with it disorder and confusion. When dying is unexpected, or there has been little time to prepare for it, disorder and confusion are almost always present.

By respecting the disorder and confusion when companioning the dying, we are honoring both the person and the finality of death itself. Instead of trying to fix what can't be fixed, we can focus our attention where it's needed – on the dying person and their needs and wishes. And, in the end, isn't that the best thing we can do?

൞ ൠ

> "Compassionate curiosity; it is not about expertise."
> ~ Dr. Wolfelt, *Companioning the Bereaved*

In addition to our desire to want to fix a bad situation, it is also human nature to want to let others know that we know what we're talking about. All of us are experts on something, and – if we're being honest with ourselves – it feels good to share our know-how with others. Especially if we think they need it!

For me, the tender truth of compassionate curiosity in the company of someone who is dying is – as the medical profession is taught – to first do no harm. Instead of demonstrating my expertise, I can sit and be with that person with the intention of listening empathically to what they are sharing. And, if it appears the dying person is interested in a conversation about what's on their mind, I can lovingly and gently ask questions that allow them to further explore what they've been saying.

Silence can be, and often is, uncomfortable. But, by remaining quiet, we frequently learn more than if we keep our minds busy with how to respond to what was just said. And, by being quiet, we're giving the dying person time to free their minds of the clutter of thoughts, and we allow them to dig as deep as they want (or need) into the topic at hand.

And, when the time seems right for a conversation, our compassionate curiosity will come across as loving and interested in what they are experiencing. Instead of coming across as all-knowing and running the risk of appearing insensitive, our compassionate curiosity offers the dying person an opportunity to heal whatever needs to be healed. After all, not all healing is physical healing.

For so many, death is seen as the enemy. I know this was the case for me when I was a paramedic and a cop. And it's certainly this way for most medical professionals – everything is done to save a person from dying. But, when a person is saved from dying, are they truly healed? It wasn't until I left the first-responder fields that I accepted for the first time in my life that death was a natural part of life. When we compassionately show curiosity, we are not only helping the dying person in their journey, but we are demonstrating to anyone else that healing doesn't always have to be physical healing. And that can be a real comfort for family and loved ones.

It takes patience, and it takes practice, but we serve the dying the best when we set aside our desire to share what we know and transform whatever knowledge we have into compassionate curiosity.

> "Companioning is about discovering the gifts of sacred silence; it is not about filling up every moment with words."
> ~ Dr. Wolfelt, *Companioning the Bereaved*

The tender truth of sacred silence with someone who is dying is knowing we don't need to pack our time with them with words; our quiet presence with that person can be the best gift we can offer.

In chaplaincy, we refer to sitting with a grieving person as the ministry of presence. There is no need to try to make the situation better or say anything at all; our simple, quiet presence can be a true gift for someone hurting. If you ask family members what they remember most about a viewing or funeral service for their loved one, the overwhelming majority would say they remember who was present – not what was said. People remember our presence more than our words. And this is never so true as with someone who is dying.

One of the biggest fears people have when asked to be with someone who is dying (or grieving) is not knowing what to say. As a minister who is often called to be with people who are hurting, and as a police chaplain whose duty it is to notify family members of the death of a loved one, I feel enormous pressure to say the right thing. When I'm asked to offer a prayer for someone who is injured or dying, I feel a need to be on my A-game. At those times, I remind myself that any comfort I can give will come from my presence, not my words.

The perfect prayer simply does not exist, but many loved ones have told me that seeing me pray silently for a family member brought them a sense of peace. Police chaplains are trained to be direct in death notifications – as gently as we can, we tell someone a loved one has died. And it's as direct as that. It's the time after that notification that our presence is most needed. In both offering a prayer and the notification of a death, it's the silence that is appreciated.

The inability to remain silent when another person is talking is perhaps the biggest obstacle to effective communication. When we're with someone dying, it's important to remember the need of that person to communicate far outweighs our desire to add our two cents. Whether sitting in silence with someone dying or remaining silent when they are talking, the sacredness of our silence will be appreciated much more than any words of wisdom we can offer.

Book Recommended by Rusty Williams

Being Mortal:
Medicine and What Matters in the End
~ Atul Gawande

The book's author, Dr. Atul Gawande, is a surgeon in Boston, Massachusetts, and a professor at Harvard Medical School. This is the first time I've heard a doctor talk about death as a natural part of life instead of the enemy that needs to be defeated. This book allowed me to not just be honest with myself but to heal wounds that had been left open since my parents died more than thirty years ago.

What resonated with me is the message to "live your best day today." Dr. Gawande describes how most people are willing to sacrifice joy today in hopes of a better tomorrow. Instead of sacrificing today, Dr. Gawande suggests that we live our best day today instead of sacrificing it in hopes of a better day tomorrow. I would assume most dying people understand this. This book opened my eyes to the importance of living this message.

About the Book

Medicine has triumphed in modern times, transforming the dangers of childbirth, injury, and disease from harrowing to manageable. But when it comes to the inescapable realities of aging and death, what medicine can do often runs counter to what it should.

Through eye-opening research and gripping stories of his own patients and family, Gawande reveals the suffering this dynamic has produced. Nursing homes, devoted above all to safety, battle with residents over the food they are allowed to eat and the choices they are allowed to make. Doctors, uncomfortable discussing patients' anxieties about death, fall back on false hopes and treatments that are actually shortening lives instead of improving them.

In his bestselling books, Atul Gawande, a practicing surgeon, has fearlessly revealed the struggles of his profession. Now he examines its ultimate limitations and failures-in his own practices as well as others' —as life draws to a close. Riveting, honest, and humane, *Being Mortal* shows how the ultimate goal is not a good death but a good life—all the way to the very end.

Rusty Williams, M.Div., D.Min.

Rusty is a police chaplain, a resiliency facilitator for first responders, and best-selling author. As a former paramedic and retired police detective, he has more than thirty years of experience in emergency services. As an ordained minister living with a spinal cord tumor, Rusty finds joy in spending time with his pets, allowing him and his wife, Elissa, to share their home in southern New Jersey.

Contact Information:
Phone: 609-975-8420
Email: 13.RWilliams@gmail.com
Website: TheBarefootMinistries.org

Reflection Questions for the Reader

What did you like best about this chapter?

What was your favorite passage in this chapter? Why did it stand out?

What feelings did this chapter evoke for you?

If you had the chance to ask the author a question, what would it be?

What form of action does this chapter inspire you to take?

What did you know about this chapter's content before you read it?

_____
_____
_____
_____
_____
_____

What new things did you learn from reading this chapter?

_____
_____
_____
_____
_____
_____

What questions do you still have?

_____
_____
_____
_____
_____
_____

What else have you read on this topic?

_____

_____

_____

_____

_____

Please visit **TenderTruthsCaringForTheDying.com** for more information, including the opportunity to meet the author during an online author and reader gathering.

CHAPTER 4

DOING "TOO MUCH" OR "NOT ENOUGH?"
Tamelynda Lux

> "Doulas can become the antidote (not the answer) to toxic stress by embodying unfaltering trust in every person's inherent wisdom and strength. We encourage a thoughtful slowing down when many feel rushed to get past a hurdle. We nurture contemplation as clients consider tumultuous questions and confusion. We turn toward and lean into suffering with our abiding faith in people."
>
> ~ Francesca Lynn Arnoldy

My caregiving relationship with my grandmother bordered on "caregiver martyrdom," at least according to her daughter, my mother. Well, my mother didn't name it caregiver martyrdom, but she clearly told me I was doing "too much."

Even though we didn't live together—my grandmother and I—while she was still living independently in her own apartment, I felt compelled to ensure she was not alone after my grandfather's passing. This meant I called her every day, took her shopping every week, accompanied her to church on Sunday mornings, and then had her spend Sunday afternoons with my husband and me at our home. I also made sure she was not alone on any statutory holidays (usually Mondays).

On one long weekend, I had a particularly upsetting conversation with my mother when I asked her if she would have my grandmother (her mother) over on that holiday Monday so she wouldn't be alone. Her tone indicated just how upset she was at my ongoing attempts to get her to provide caregiving in ways that *I* wanted her involved (more, not less) and not in the same ways *she* wanted to provide caregiving. It was an eye-opening conversation.

One tender truth of caring for the dying that many do not want to talk about is the role of caregiver martyrdom that many fall into. It is a common issue I see as a caregiver coach. I've also noticed that many do not even realize they have fallen into that role.

Caregiver martyrdom is when the caregiver *develops a martyr attitude and takes strict ownership of caregiving tasks. The caregiver* becomes so enmeshed with the needs and desires of their "person" that they neglect their own needs. *Caregiving for someone can quickly turn into a sense of identity for the caregiver. These "selfless" caregivers often pay a high price when taking on this role, suffering from sadness, depression, and isolation, among other things.*

Caregiver martyrs tend to:

- have a strong urge and need to feel needed,
- refuse to let siblings or other family participate in caregiving, and
- complain that they get no help.

The martyr complex pattern of behavior is characterized by self-sacrifice and service to others. Identifying this trait can help prevent burnout or undue stress on relationships. While some aspects of martyrdom may appear to be noble and honorable, it is essential to acknowledge the negative consequences.

The negative consequences of caregiver martyrdom can be experienced quickly or slowly, similar to that of a life-sucking funnel, and include:

- loss of interest in activities,
- withdrawal from friends and family,
- feeling hopeless and helpless,
- changes in appetite and weight,
- changes in sleep patterns,
- increase in illnesses,
- exhaustion—emotionally and physically,
- use of alcohol or drugs as coping devices, and
- feelings of self-harm or wanting to do harm to others.

Where does the desire to become entwined with a dying person's needs and desires come from? It comes from codependence, guilt, and ego, to name a few.

Codependence occurs when one partner is reliant on the other and vice versa. This cyclical relationship is the foundation of what experts mean when they speak of the "cycle" of codependency. The only source of self-esteem and self-worth for a codependent is sacrificing for their partner, who is only too happy to accept their sacrifices, as described in an article by *Medical News Today*.

I don't recall being in that cycle, but my self-esteem did seem tied up with what I could do for my grandmother. My self-esteem was also tied up in how my mother perceived my involvement or rather "over-involvement" with my grandmother. A lot of this has since been resolved thanks to a caring therapist who helped me understand its origins and find self-esteem in healthier ways.

Another root of the caregiving martyr complex is guilt. And according to Shawn Wilburn (LaShawn Splane-Wilburn), founder of Homagi, a non-profit assisting and supporting caregivers caring for loved ones with mental health disorders, "Feeling ashamed for putting parents into nursing homes to be cared for more thoroughly becomes a dreadful thought. Who wants to be viewed as neglecting, or worse yet, abandoning their parents? Some caregivers fear being seen as incapable of caring for their parents effectively and therefore see asking for help as a failure on their part. I can relate to this feeling of being seen as neglecting my loved one if I didn't do it all."

My grandmother eventually entered long-term care, and at first, I felt guilty that I didn't take her in with us. But I had experienced that years before, having had my mother-in-law live with us until it was absolutely clear we could no longer care for her. My relationship with my mother-in-law changed when she lived with us, and we became her daily caregivers—it wasn't all roses. My grandmother and I spoke about her potentially moving in with my husband and me, and we agreed it would not work.

Ego is another contributor to the complexity that makes up caregiver martyrdom syndrome. Typically, caregiving usually goes to the geographically closest child. I've learned from client conversations that many siblings in that role do not give their other siblings a chance to participate in caregiving. According to Carol Bradley Bursack, a veteran family caregiver who spent more than two decades caring for a total of seven elders, "This is where the ego rises, which loves the attention and sympathy received from friends, neighbors, and coworkers." Having siblings involved or accepting their help makes it harder for the primary caregiving sibling to complain and lessens the praise for being selfless, so other family members are either kept at arm's length or in the dark.

Another interesting concept that contributes to caregiver martyrdom is the victim role. According to a *WebMD* article, the medical community believes that there is a link between the martyr and victim roles, which are closely related because they share similar motives, conditions, and behavior. "At its core, the victim complex involves someone viewing themselves as a victim of their life events. They often express that bad things always happen to them, claim that they have no control over their life, and don't take responsibility for things they do. The motives for a victim mentality are often unconscious." This is something I frequently find in posts on support groups on social media, where someone laments their caregiving position and, for every suggestion offered, there's a reason why it can't be done.

Although the root cause of a caregiver's martyr tendencies may be complex, it is not impossible to overcome them. And while it is challenging being a caregiver, it can be even more difficult realizing you need to ask for help for yourself, as Beverly and Jack each experienced in their lives.

Beverly had reached the end of her rope one day in being the sole caregiver for her husband. One of Beverly's trusted siblings, who was aware of the situation, called social services, who assigned a caseworker to Beverly's husband and Beverly. The husband wasn't too happy, felt he was "getting better," and did not want a carer. The husband insisted on only wanting Beverly, who had finally recognized her need to have someone come in so that she could have a breather now and then. Beverly also knew she needed to stick to her guns on this because she was exhausted. Her husband tried to keep her hooked 100 percent in the very demanding role of caregiver, despite her exhaustion. It would take a period of adjustment, but with Beverly continuing to assert herself with her husband and "stick to her guns," the situation would change, and the strain on Beverly would shift for the better. An understanding and experienced support like a social worker in this instance helped.

In another completely different family and scenario, Jack mentioned that he and his sibling took care of their parents for years and only called in hospice support in the last couple of months before the parents passed away. He explained how hard the decision was but needed it because they could no longer do everything the parents needed help with. By getting outside help, the two siblings could keep their parents at home and out of a long-term care facility, and they were at home when they passed. Jack said he had a hard time making the decision to get outside help, but by bringing in support, he and his sibling could provide for their parents what everyone wanted—care at home and death not in an institution but at home.

It breaks my heart to see a caregiver suffering, and the question I have asked is, *Why? Why is this caregiver suffering?* Life is too short to be suffering.

I can appreciate it when there is no extended family or friends to call on. I mean because they literally do not exist. And I can appreciate the difficulty of getting home care services. Even before the pandemic, there were problems with getting personal support workers to provide people with the help they needed at home. The crisis in home care continues to be reported by the media. That is sad but what is really sad to me is when caregivers choose to add limitations such as saying no to options that are clearly possible in terms of providing support to them. I am not saying it's easy, but it is doable.

In my own life, I would most likely have tumbled deeper into caregiver martyrdom had it not been for my mother telling me that what I was doing for my grandmother was "too much." At first, I was offended; thought she just didn't understand and was jealous of my relationship with my grandmother. And maybe she was. But as I thought about my own health and well-being, I realized there was some truth to what she was saying. I'm thankful that conversation happened because I ultimately chose a different way of caregiving. The different way was *my way*, what felt doable to me.

> **"Some caregivers believe they are the *only* ones who can care properly for their family member."**
> ~ AGEugate

When a caregiver martyr believes they are the *only* one who can properly care for their person, they typically:

- believe other family members and friends are "inadequate" to care for their person, with resentment and anger often stirring among the caring circle,
- take on more and more responsibility, often to the detriment of their own needs or those of their family, and
- isolate themselves and their person from those who are willing and able to help in the care of that individual.

It's a snowball effect of emotion, responsibility, and isolation. Just imagine your own situation for a moment.

- Who in your family or friend circle could provide adequate care for your person? And when were the last ten times that happened?
- What responsibilities from the list of daily and occasional tasks can you shift to someone else? Who can you shift them to?
- What activities have you done outside of the home alone or with your person that weren't directly healthcare-related but more social in nature? List the last five occasions.

Maybe you are like I was at one point thinking it was just so much easier for me to do "everything" because there was so much to organize—medications, hygiene items, meals—and then writing out instructions to ensure everything would be done "just right" and perfectly. After all, if things weren't, I would pay the price later. The price later would be me on the receiving end of agitated behavior or outbursts of anger, not sleeping, not eating, and the possible health decline of my grandmother. The possibilities are endless in an overreactive caregiver martyr's mindset.

But as I pulled back just a little from the all-consuming caregiving role that I took on, I felt the benefit of the "time off." The benefit to me was a reduced feeling of being "squeezed to death by a python" (as much as I loved my grandmother), and as a result, I had more physical, mental, and emotional ability to breathe more freely. This freedom to breathe more easily meant my marriage wasn't suffering, and I could be a better caregiver to my grandmother.

What I have found interesting since my experience with my grandmother is that practitioners can also experience caregiver martyr syndrome. Let me repeat that. *Practitioners can also experience caregiver martyr syndrome.*

For palliative care specialists and end-of-life doulas, the common goal is to provide comfort care for those suffering from a terminal illness and during their active dying journey. As end-of-life practitioners, we benefit from being emotionally strong and knowing when to set boundaries. This may not be an easy task since we are guiding people through one of the most difficult times of their lives, and we want to be there for them. It can be immensely rewarding work, but I cannot state enough how important it is to set and keep boundaries.

Whether a formal end-of-life practitioner or an informal caregiver, there are five areas to consider when assessing if you are tumbling into caregiver martyr syndrome.

1. The "feel-good" of sacrifice. If you are making sacrifices because doing so makes you feel good, and you are not doing it for career recognition, then there may be a problem. The common response to praise or thanks for one's sacrifice for a caregiver martyr is, "Oh, it was nothing," dismissing the action. If you find yourself saying making the sacrifice, whatever it was, is unimportant, I encourage you to give your actions some thought.

If you are a chronic giver, you may want to re-examine why you are sacrificing so much. Assess if you are crossing your boundaries. If you don't have boundaries for yourself, set them and adhere to them. Writing those boundaries down on a note you can post somewhere visible at home can be a helpful reminder as you learn to stick to your boundaries. Doing things for others should not be more important than your own needs. You might find that you are sacrificing for someone else's needs, and if you find that you do this regularly and you want to live a healthier, more balanced life, it is time to change.

2. Doing "everything" and solving everyone's problems. Attempting to be a hero for everyone, especially without complaint, is a slippery slope into the depths of caregiver martyr syndrome.

We often think we can solve all the world's problems by doing everything, but it does not work that way. The consequences of doing everything can be significant. Is it really worth it? The answer depends on how you view things. Know that resentment can build both in others (you may be perceived as that infamous "fixer" or worse, "control freak") and yourself. There is a way out of this trap of doing "everything" or "solving everyone's problem" so that you can live a more balanced, healthier life.

3. Personal health is slipping. We know how important self-care is because we also know that when one's cup is empty, there is nothing to give. Changes in personal hygiene and health are clear signs of a martyr complex.

There is growing concern about the eroding health of caregivers, both formal and informal, because of their neglect to their own well-being. And often, this can be seriously life-threatening. Caregivers frequently face decreased motivation and efficiency and may have complaints—usually unexpressed—about their role in providing care. Additionally, caregivers may experience chronic physical and mental symptoms and become increasingly withdrawn and unpleasant in communication. If you notice any of these signs, seek help.

The eroding health of caregivers can affect any area of one's life. Positive relationships can alleviate some of the subjective burden, but caregivers need more than just social support and a supportive role.

4. Seeking opportunities to sacrifice. When a person looks for ways to step into harm's way, this is a red flag similar to thoughts of self-harm.

The concept of victim mentality comes up when looking at self-sacrifice. People with a victim mentality use passive aggression to get attention and justify their behavior. They also avoid subjects that upset them. It is exhausting to live with such a mentality. When will it be time to stop enabling this type of mentality and make life a little easier? While it may be in one's nature to reject offers of help, content with feeling sorry for oneself, it is not healthy. You can begin by changing the way you think about yourself. Take a deep breath and reach out to a therapist, another practitioner in a formal coaching role, or a hypnotherapist (my specialty).

5. Personal values and unrealistic priorities. Some caregivers feel that their actions are an expression of how much they care. And they feel that if they are not working hard for people, it means they don't have compassion or care or love them enough. How do you express and demonstrate love? Is how you are conveying love something that needs shifting?

It is possible to break out of the caregiver martyr role. Learning how to deal with the effects of martyrdom can help you prevent future problems.

1. Recognize there are *options*, and you have a *choice*.

There are *always* options. Sometimes we just cannot see them ourselves. And there may be people in your life who cannot or will not help you in the way you need or want. This is where having a trusted friend, therapist, pastor, peer, or end-of-life practitioner can be helpful.

And then there is the *choice*. There is the choice to truly delve into whatever options seem appropriate or best for the situation. If the option does not pan out, try another way. Reframe the mindset from "It won't work" to "How *can* I make this work? What *can* I do in whole or part to make this work?"

2. Express your needs.

Time and time again, I talk about the inability of others to read our minds or read between the lines of any passive-aggressive comment and that we must explicitly and kindly tell them what it is we want them to know. It is vital to clearly tell people what you want and need.

Caregivers with siblings who are not helping would benefit from looking at their own part in creating the dynamic for this to occur. My intention is to nudge and encourage you to secure the assistance and reinforcement you want and need, which is healthy to have from time to time. If siblings are not geographically close enough to help, they can help in other ways: financially or in other remote ways. It is a matter of getting creative on what the other ways of remote support look like.

As Carol Bradley Bursack says in *Minding Our Elders*, siblings often don't help because they assume that the sibling closest to the dying individual has things under control. More often than not, they do not have any idea about what is involved—time, effort, and sacrifice—in caregiving. So be clear on what you want and need, write *everything* down on a list, and choose which activities or support can be done by someone remotely.

Some would say you just need to ask and hope they hear it but let me offer this guidance: Tell them what you need, what is important about it, when you need it by, and deliver a call-to-action statement to get a firm commitment from them. At first, this may feel very strange, but with practice, you will feel more comfortable with the phrasing and the asking.

The Start of the Request	Example
What I need is . . .	you to come and sit with Helga from 10:00 a.m. to 2:00 p.m. on Sunday [date].
This is important to me because . . .	I need a break and need to get out of the house for a few hours.
I need it by . . .	Sunday is important because I have made plans to look after myself for a few hours. *(No need to explain any further.)*
Will you do this for me?	*Use silence and wait.*

3. Set boundaries

When beginning to express your needs, you may experience fear of rejection. And some people may respond with incredulity or anger when you set boundaries, but most people will adjust to reasonable requests. It is a matter of you maintaining assertive and clear communication. Psychologist Rachel Zoffness in her article "How to Set Boundaries With Family," offers the following guide for setting healthy boundaries with family. Granted, she suggests this during the holidays, but it is also appropriate for setting boundaries in general.

- <u>Value yourself and your time</u>. If you do not value how you spend your time, no one else will. Dive deep into what matters to you and what your life values are.
- <u>Give yourself permission to do what's best for you</u>. You are your biggest advocate and support. Regardless of whether or not others understand and accept them, it is important to

have healthy boundaries. Limiting or deleting time with toxic people is an act of self-love.

- <u>Know your triggers and anticipate them</u>. A trigger is a situation or event that sets off negative emotions or unwanted actions. Be one step ahead of your triggers by knowing what they are, the emotions that arise, how to take care of yourself when they arise, and how you plan to respond.

- <u>Be clear about your needs and communicate them</u>. Identify your needs and boundaries in advance. Write them down on a list. Once you've identified them, communicate them assertively, not aggressively, in a kind and clear manner.

- <u>Practice saying no</u>. There are soft no's (they leave room for a potential yes in the future) and hard no's (they are firm and finite). You can shift any habitual people-pleasing once you understand your boundaries and how to say no.

- <u>Make a list of coping strategies</u>. By creating a list in advance, when those times of feeling isolated or complicated come up (and they will), you will have a go-to strategy to better manage the situations. I made a long list of activities ranging from individual household tasks to specific people to reach out to for outdoor activities.

When I think about caregiving for my grandmother, I think there were times when I was "doing too much" and "not doing enough" *for myself*. Life is short. Being a caregiver martyr might make life even shorter. Just imagine all the life you would miss if you only focused on caring for others and not for yourself. My wish for everyone is to journey well—as well as you can.

REFERENCES

Medical News Today. May 27, 2022.

Medically reviewed by Dan Brennan, MD. "What is a Martyr Complex?" *WebMD*. October 25, 2021.

Self-Care Tip

Take time. Take time to *prepare yourself* for your client visit. Take time to *decompress* after a client visit. I have a short ceremony and prayer I do before each client session or visit. And after the session or visit, I go for a walk down my long laneway—whether it's summer or winter—which gives me time to process what happened; I process what occurred for the client but, more importantly, what happened for *me*.

Tip or Strategy to Help Other Practitioners or Caregivers

Streamline and automate your administrative activities as much as possible! Color coding my files and organizing paperwork helps me stay on top of things. It works for both the business of being a practitioner as well as caregiving for my loved one.

My website is set up through GoDaddy with an online calendar connected automatically to set up Zoom meetings. I'm taking as much manual administration as possible out of everyday tasks. By using an online calendar with a notification feature, I get text reminders on my phone about an upcoming session or appointment. I even plug in my appointments (massage, doctor, hair, etc.) so that I get a reminder notification one hour before any appointment. This helps me tremendously. I also keep a paper-based calendar and write everything in there too.

Have a good therapist on speed dial *for yourself* for those more challenging times when you don't want to tap into your peer group, as helpful and loving as they are. Also, know your resources and referral sources in a separate speed dial system so you can easily refer clients or inquiries as appropriate.

Something I Wish I'd Known When I Began This Journey as a Practitioner in End-of-Life Care and What I Discovered

I wish I'd known how I would be impacted so deeply by this work. Okay, I expected some impact and assumed with all the personal work I'd done over the years (inner child work, parts therapy, talk therapy, and end-of-life scenarios and case studies), I would be able to "handle it." But I misled myself. I didn't realize there could be something that would trigger an old memory or hurt or wound or that grief and loss that never really "goes away."

ℰᎡ

> **"Companioning is about compassionate curiosity; it is not about expertise."**
> ~ Dr. Wolfelt, *Companioning the Bereaved*

Going deeper into end-of-life conversations can expose what's hidden beneath the surface and foster greater awareness for the client. It can also foster closeness and connection between the client and practitioner.

Long before I became an end-of-life doula, I became a certified Co-Active Professional Coach. I learned the value of bringing active listening, bold questions, intuition, and other skills to every connection.

In my end-of-life work, I use co-active coaching approaches in various ways, one of which is to deepen interpersonal ties by remaining alert and asking kind, compassionate questions. Curiosity, not authority, inspires openness, which encourages self-reflection.

Book Recommended by Tamelynda Lux

52 McGs.
The Best Obituaries from Legendary
New York Times Writer Robert McG. Thomas Jr.
~ Robert McG. Thomas Jr.

I don't read the local (or any) obituaries on a regular basis; I only read them when someone I know has died. However, this book intrigued me.

The obituaries are like short stories about people's lives—fascinating. The stories remind me that people are more than who is presented (physically) in front of me. Everyone has a history. And I believe everyone's life history is filled with dreams, milestones, successes and failures, and learnings. That's what life is.

Every day and especially in our practices as end-of-life doulas, we meet interesting non-famous people who spent part (or all) of their lives doing things that impacted others' lives, maybe even society's. This is important to me because I want to honor, respect, value, and show appreciation for the people I meet.

About the Book

Among his devoted fans, his pieces were known simply as McGs. With a "genius for illuminating that sometimes ephemeral apogee in people's lives when they prove capable of generating a brightly burning spark" (Columbia Journalism Review), Robert McG. Thomas Jr. commemorated fascinating, unconventional lives with signature style and wit.

Thomas captured life's ironies and defining moments with elegance and a gift for making a sentence sing. He had an uncanny sense of the passion and personality that make each life unique, and the ability, as Joseph Epstein wrote, to "look beyond the facts and the rigid formula of the obit to touch on a deeper truth."

Tamelynda Lux, CCH, PCC, DipAdEd

With over 30 years of experience, Tamelynda has invested her career in supporting individuals as a life coach and then evolved her private practice to include hypnosis for life issues and concerns, end-of-life support, and grief coaching.

Certified in the specialty of End-of-Life Hypnosis and as an End-of-Life Doula, Tamelynda provides non-medical, holistic support to the dying person and/or their family. She is a Certified End-of-Life Doula, Certified Psychological First Aid (Instructor Level) Canadian Red Cross, and has completed Certified Mental Health First Aid with the Canadian Mental Health Association.

Tamelynda is actively involved with the aging population, including as a community member on the board of a non-profit for Alzheimer's and dementia, with a day program and long-term care residence.

Contact Information:
Phone: 519-670-5219
Email: info@TamelyndaLux.com
Website: www.TamelyndaLux.com
Mailing: PO Box 29061, London, Ontario N6K 4L9 Canada

Reflection Questions for the Reader

What did you like best about this chapter?

What was your favorite passage in this chapter? Why did it stand out?

What feelings did this chapter evoke for you?

If you had the chance to ask the author a question, what would it be?

What form of action does this chapter inspire you to take?

What did you know about this chapter's content before you read it?

What new things did you learn from reading this chapter?

What questions do you still have?

What else have you read on this topic?

_____
_____
_____
_____
_____
_____

Please visit **TenderTruthsCaringForTheDying.com** for more information, including the opportunity to meet the author during an online author and reader gathering.

CHAPTER 5

JUST BREATHE
Brenda Hennessey

> "In order to understand the dance, one must be still.
> And in order to truly understand the stillness,
> one must dance."
>
> ~ Rumi

When I met Betty, it was summer, and she was always keen to spend some time outside if it wasn't too hot. She was in her seventies and had cancer.

Betty was one of the first residents in the three-room residential hospice with whom I became close. The hospice featured two big doors in each resident's room, allowing us to easily maneuver the resident to the outside patio.

When Betty first entered the hospice, she could walk a short distance with her walker and sit in the reclining chair in her room. Betty could still use her walker to get outside and ultimately rest on its seat or sit in her reclining chair in her room. At least for the first few times I visited her. She loved the sunshine; we would both shut our eyes and allow the sun to heat our faces. She told me that it always felt good to her and, I confess, it also did to me.

I got to know Betty by asking her some of the questions we were taught to ask when training as an end-of-life doula "How did you meet your husband?" "Tell me, what made you fall in love with him?" "Tell me about your children." "What was it like when you were a child?" She happily shared her answers and, at times, seemed surprised that I wanted to hear about her life. Betty would say, "I'm not anybody special. Why would you want to hear about me?" And I would tell her that even though she may not realize it, her life and story were special and important. She would smile and tell me how nice I was to her.

Over the next couple of visits, Betty grew much weaker. She could no longer use her walker, but we made sure that we got her outside when the weather permitted. Opening the double doors in her room, we rolled her out to the patio in her hospital bed.

Our time together got quieter but no less meaningful. I spent time holding her hand in comfort, massaging her dry, fragile skin with lotion, and just sitting with her so when she did awaken, she was not alone. I could feel my sadness as I knew my new friend's time was limited. Often, I sat quietly with her, saying nothing, reflecting on the stories she had shared about her life, feeling such honor that she had shared them with me. My heart felt such gratitude.

The last night I sat with Betty was the hardest of all. She was restless and calling out for her husband, who had passed some time before. I worked to find ways to comfort her, asking her what she needed and letting her know I was there with her and that she was not alone. Betty looked at me with tears and said she didn't want to do this anymore. She asked me when it was going to end. My intuitive answer—the only one I had—was, "Soon, Betty." I sensed her exhaustion. The fight to stay on this earth was becoming too much for her failing body.

I felt an uneasiness in my body, knowing that we were moving closer to Betty dying. I also felt the helplessness I had felt years before when my parents died. I knew that to work through my feelings and provide compassionate and loving care to Betty, I needed to open my heart wider and allow it to guide me as I assisted her on her journey.

Both my parents died in their mid-fifties from cancer. My mother was diagnosed with glioblastoma ten weeks from diagnosis to death. Shy of three years after my mother's death, my father was diagnosed with adenocarcinoma and died four weeks later. I experienced the overwhelmingness of sitting in cold, sterile hospital rooms, being told by a physician that my loved ones had each been diagnosed with an incurable illness. The shock, the darkness of disbelief, the vibration of my heart pounding through my chest, and the horrific thought of my normal, stable world as I knew it was no longer.

My parents experienced weeks, not months or years, from diagnosis to death. I questioned my faith at the time—was there really a God? If so, why would he take both my parents? What did I do to deserve this punishment? So much anger and sadness enveloped me.

Back then, death in our family was not discussed, advance care planning was not even heard of, and palliative or hospice care did not exist in our small town. The doctors did not relay to us that my mother or father were going to die, only that there was little hope for any type of treatment. We were left floundering on our own, trying to understand exactly what it was they were carefully telling us. We needed answers from the medical team as to any treatment options, the success of those treatments, and what to expect if treatment was unsuccessful. It was extremely frustrating for my family, having no medical background, being in shock, in fear, vulnerable, and doing our best to navigate a care system we knew nothing about.

It had been almost thirty years since their deaths as I sat with Betty.

The nursing team had given Betty medication to ease her symptoms and help make her comfortable. I did my best to comfort

Betty by holding her hand, gently wiping her tears from her cheeks, and silently sitting with her. This was all I could do or knew how to do for her. Betty was dying, and we all cared for her with compassion, dignity, and grace.

I was not with Betty when she died. I received an email from the hospice advising me that she had transitioned the next day peacefully, with her family by her side. I felt a sense of relief that she no longer had to endure her unwanted lingering. Her journey here on earth was complete, and I sat quietly, holding her memory and sending her love. I felt gratitude for the privilege of getting to know Betty, spending time, and caring for her, yet I also felt sadness for my loss of a new friend.

Caring for the dying is one of the most challenging yet fulfilling roles we can do. Most of us who feel drawn to end-of-life work have experienced a loss of our own. It may have been the sudden death or a drawn-out illness of a loved one that has led us to this path of caring for the dying.

Having cared for my dying parents inspired me to support others and their families during their time of such stress, upheaval, uncertainty, and vulnerability, a role that I am grateful for. I feel called to this role as a compassionate helper, empathetic listener, and truthful supporter to the individual dying and their loved ones. I honor the dying's wishes, fears, and vulnerability without judgment but with kindness and importance, asking my own beliefs to stay silent.

Providing guidance and knowledge to those on their end-of-life journey and their loved ones provides them comfort in understanding their wishes for care will be met in the best possible way. This allows the dying and their loved ones to focus on what's meaningful during this last bit of time together.

Caring for the dying moved me to open my heart with compassion for myself. Engaging in this work can be both exhausting and energizing at the same time. Our emotions and energy can be heavy and draining. They can also be light with joyfulness and serenity. End-of-life work can awaken feelings and sensations in our bodies that we may have not felt in a long time or perhaps never before. It nudges us to visit with these new or resurfaced emotions, be curious, ask ourselves questions, listen and reflect within, and give ourselves the compassionate care we, too, deserve.

Finding and spending time with our tribe is a supporting way to share how we manage our self-care. Our tribe provides the understanding and safe container, allowing us to be vulnerable, listen to our challenges openly without judgment, and ask for help or advice if needed, thus creating wonderful friendships.

As a newer death doula and hospice volunteer, I have questioned my ability to be in this role. We doubt ourselves and are sometimes hesitant to act as we feel. We may do or say the wrong thing to the resident and/or their loved ones. We don't know everything, and that's okay. We don't have to.

Ask them questions: Do they want to be touched? Would they like to listen to a certain genre of music? Do they enjoy watching specific television shows? Do they like to look out the window or prefer the blinds drawn? Each individual we care for is unique, and the best way to support their end-of-life care is to learn what brings them comfort. We learn through asking, doing, experiencing, and reflecting. I believe that if we open our hearts and allow our intuition to guide us, we will offer authentic, dignified, and compassionate care.

Talking about death has become comfortable for me. I talk about it a lot. My son will often comment, "Mom, why do you always talk about death?" My response is always the same, "It will happen to all of us, and there's no stopping it."

My experience of caring for my parents during their illness and dying has given me an understanding of how important it is to educate others about our choices regarding end-of-life care. I feel moved to share my experience and encourage others to begin to think about and envision what their dying might look like.

Advanced care planning is important at any age or stage in our lives, not just for the elderly. Sudden accidents or illnesses happen at any time to those we love and even ourselves. How will we know the care our loved ones wish for if we do not open ourselves up to have these uncomfortable conversations? How will my loved ones know the care or wishes for my dying if I don't tell them?

Many of us have likely been affected by the sudden illness or death of a loved one and have felt the helplessness of not knowing what to do, struggled with a heart-wrenching decision needing to be made, and perhaps felt guilt over that decision. Making time to dive into these important conversations regarding end-of-life care before we are immersed in the shock of a terminal diagnosis or the phone call advising of a horrible accident is one of the most cherished precious gifts we can give to our loved ones.

We need to encourage and advocate for people to share their thoughts on how they wish to be cared for, digging into the specifics of what treatment would be acceptable or not, and who they trust to be their substitute decision-maker if they lose the capacity to communicate their wishes directly—do they wish to die at home if possible—and compassionately understand their reasoning for their decisions and respecting these without judgment.

The more conversations loved ones have about their end-of-life journey, the more helpful it is to those that may ultimately be faced with the challenge of making these decisions. The wishes of their loved ones can be given, as best as possible, through awareness of what is important to the dying person, helping their loved ones lessen the uncertainty and possible guilt of making the wrong decision. Advance care planning is one of the greatest gifts we can give our loved ones.

When twilight pulls the curtain down and pins it with a star,
Remember that you have a friend no matter where you are.
~ A poem from my mother's high school autograph book

Self-Care Tip

Do what makes you feel joy. As a caregiver, I can become involved and spend all my time tending to those who need my support and care. Finding time to look after me is important and necessary to my well-being.

Many times we hear, "You need to look after yourself first, or you're no good to others," or "Put your oxygen mask on first." Yes, we all know this, but what does looking after ourselves really mean?

We are all unique individuals, and some of us know exactly what our soul needs. It may be a daily meditation practice, a hot bath with a glass of wine, and a good book. If you're unsure what that means to you, do what brings you joy.

I have learned to take the time needed to do whatever allows me to stop and feel joy. It may be as simple as taking a few minutes to sit outside in the warmth of the sun on a bright winter day, playing with my furry loved one, or having a water fight with my kids on a hot summer day. I don't feel compelled to explain or describe it or tell anyone what it is. Some days I just want to feel like a kid again and play and allow myself to take the time, even if it's only a few minutes a day or a week, to do just that—play, smile, laugh, feel happiness and gratitude in my heart. My mantra is: Whatever you need, do what makes you feel joy.

Tip or Strategy to Help Other Practitioners or Caregivers

Find your tribe.

Having a small group of friends and/or peers with similar interests and goals is so helpful. They can be your trusted resource when you need advice, a tender ear when you need someone to listen to how tough your day was, and a true friend to have a giggle or two over a glass of wine at the end of a week.

Something I Wish I'd Known When I Began This Journey as a Practitioner in End-of-Life Care and What I Discovered

I didn't know I'd be part of such an awesome end-of-life care network. When I began, I was concerned that I might have difficulty as I don't have a medical care background, and it appeared many others did. The group of individuals I am connected to is amazing and has been so welcoming and kind. End-of-life care practitioners have had careers in different fields, including medicine or social work, and I believe most have had a loss in their lives, leading them to this work.

I have also had the privilege of meeting and learning from inspiring mentors, teachers, and peers. There is no competition in this field as we all work together to foster discussions about death and dying, increase the awareness of choices for end-of-life care, the many community supports available to the individuals and their families, and the importance of advance care planning including for each of us. I am grateful to be part of this life-changing hard-working network.

I didn't realize how sharing in someone's end-of-life journey would be such an honor. It is always lovely to hear a resident's family say, "She's really nice, isn't she?" when I leave the resident's room at the hospice. I feel that even the little things I do or say helps them, perhaps by putting a smile on their face or giving them the space they need to talk, listening, and not judging. I am grateful to have this opportunity to share the end-of-life journey with every dear soul I have the privilege to care for, hear stories of their lives, and spend time with them and their family as they transition.

> **"Listening with the heart; it is not about analyzing with the head."**
> ~ Dr. Wolfelt, *Companioning the Bereaved*

Listening with the heart is so important. We are respecting their wishes with no judgment, only compassion. By being present with them, we can stay in the current moment and hold space for the stories that are being shared, understand, and reflect on the feelings they are identifying through their words or physical expression as they speak. We can notice the vulnerability of the residents or the loved ones we're caring for and provide empathy and support in listening. Pausing and providing silence is a way of listening from the heart as it allows us to continue to stay in the moment. Silence or pausing can be uncomfortable or scary for some, though.

In our busy lives, daily, there's so much commotion, much going on, and many thoughts flowing in and out of our minds that once you stop the thought process, be still, and in the moment, silence can be a beautiful thing. Getting past the uncomfortableness of the pause or the silence can be difficult for some, yet once they can settle the commotion, they recognize calmness. At the hospice, some residents embrace the silence. I am even guilty of going into a resident's room and thinking, *Gee. It's quiet in here. There's no TV on.* Through my learnings of being an end-of-life doula, we focus on what the client would like, so I begin considering whether or not they like music. Music can be more soothing for some, and I'll ask them if they would like some music on? Sometimes they do, yet I find they are content with the quiet more often than not.

I believe residents are sometimes lonely if they haven't had many visitors. They welcome hearing the voices of others within the hospice, whether it's the care team, the other residents and their visitors, or even day-to-day happenings of the phone or main door ringing. I think it helps them feel like they are a part of a social connection, a community that may be lacking when they're in their room.

When we're able to go in and spend time with someone at their end of life, I always make sure that I'm grounding myself, quieting my mind, and not having any expectation of how the visit is going to go as I very much wish for it to be organic. My aim is to be open, listen from my heart, and let them lead the conversation if they feel like talking or sharing. Otherwise, many times it's sitting, being present so they are not alone, being silent, and holding comforting space.

It's such a beautiful experience to share this journey with someone. When we're new at companioning, it's scary. We have a fear of not knowing what to expect. We have doubts about being capable of supporting the resident or client and doing the job well. We are also vulnerable to allowing ourselves to open and discover what we don't know. I have found that by allowing myself to just go with the flow, listen, and speak from my heart, I learn so much more about what I can do than I could have ever imagined.

We have many learnings in our lifetime. And although we might not agree with people's choices or the way that they want, or even the family might want the person to have some type of treatment or some type of care, is being able to navigate some conflict. I don't like conflict. It's a heavy word. Perhaps it's better to say "some disagreement" of that care and learn to be supportive to the family, the resident, or the client.

For example, I've seen different times where we struggle, or the family struggles with life-prolonging care versus what the resident or client wishes. How do we navigate that line? That difference? And how can we bring understanding to both sides in a way that will bring love, support, and sometimes courage to the loved ones? We can learn much from others in how they think, feel, and care for the person, their loved one, and their dying. We benefit from ensuring we're open to all of that, to fully have the compassion, the understanding, the digging into the feelings, the fears, and the reasoning, helping them work through some of that themselves and bring everyone together as best we can.

We had a family recently that was very much struggling with this. And I had the privilege to work with the caregivers at the hospice and to dialogue, reflect, come back, and talk more. Just that back and forth, we eventually all got to where the family agreed. And that's a difficult situation.

My initial thought in the situation was that this person is in their dying, *transitioning. Why would anyone want to prolong that?* And that's where judgment comes in. That's where our own opinion comes in. So, my learning through this was having experienced a situation with the death of my mother where I got to the point that I understood our wish for her was not to be in that space any longer because we felt it was not fair for what she would like. We can be quick to say, "Oh, you don't want that for your person." Or "Oh, you don't really want . . ." But that's not what to do, right? It is better to dig into it, dig a little deeper, investigate, and listen with the heart to realize the feelings and emotions that the loved ones are experiencing and provide them the safe container to work through their thoughts. So, take the time and listen with the heart.

I need to take *my* expectation, and *my* belief, and *my* thought right out of the equation and listen with *my heart*.

Book Recommended by Brenda Hennessey

Top Five Regrets of the Dying: A Life Transformed by the Dearly Departing
~ Bronnie Ware

When I began thinking about the reality of becoming a caregiver for individuals at their end of life, I discovered this book. Or, more precisely, perhaps it found its way to me. I purchased the book and read it in five days which was pretty impressive for me as I hadn't read an entire book in years!

The first of the top five regrets of the dying Bronnie Ware identifies is "I wish I'd had the courage to live a life true to myself, not the life others expected of me." Wow, this hit me hard. I read it again. It was like a huge lightning bolt struck me, and I was filled with electricity. The realization that I was doing this exact thing was shocking. So now what? Not able to put the book down, I continued reading.

It was time for me to be honest with myself and everyone in my family that *my* life would change. Some may like the changes I would make and embrace them; others may hate them and be judgemental. It didn't matter. I had to start the journey of discovering who I was, where my belief patterns of what I "should do" in life came from, unlock the chains from the cage I had put myself in, and transition into the beautiful soul that was put on this earth for a reason.

I am empowered to live my life regret-free.

About the Book

After too many years of unfulfilling work, Bronnie Ware began searching for a job with heart. Despite having no formal qualifications or previous experience in the field, she found herself working in palliative care. During the time she spent tending to those who were dying, Bronnie's life was transformed. Later, she wrote an Internet blog post outlining the most common regrets that the people she had cared for had expressed. The post gained so much momentum that it was viewed by more than three million readers worldwide in its first year. At the request of many, Bronnie subsequently wrote a book, *The Top Five Regrets of the Dying*, to share her story.

Bronnie has had a colorful and diverse life. By applying the lessons of those nearing their death to her own life, she developed an understanding that it is possible for everyone, if we make the right choices, to die with peace of mind.

In this revised edition of the best-selling memoir that has been read by over a million people worldwide, with translations in 29 languages, Bronnie expresses how significant these regrets are and how we can positively address these issues while we still have the time. *The Top Five Regrets of the Dying* gives hope for a better world. It is a courageous, life-changing book that will leave you feeling more compassionate and inspired to live the life you are truly here to live.

Book Recommended by Brenda Hennessey

Embraced by the Light: The Most Profound and Complete Near-Death Experience Ever
~ Betty J. Eadie

After my mother died, my aunt told me that I needed to read this book. She was a kind lady yet could be very pushy, and at that time, I didn't want to take much advice from anyone, especially her. After my dad died, she told me I needed to read this book again. I gave in, read the book, and was grateful to her for being pushy.

Betty J. Eadie described her near-death experience in a way that I connected with and enlightened me to a spiritual understanding that I was unaware of—soul contracts. The author shared that before our soul comes to earth for our lessons, our family members, friends, and partners know each other and agree to our "life plans," our soul contracts. Even though we don't remember what our soul already knows when we get to earth, every part of our life is planned, leading us to the situations where we learn the lessons required to fulfill our contracts. Even our deaths are planned.

Reading this book helped me see our lives in a completely different understanding. Knowing my parents as I did, I felt peace and comfort, believing they lived the life they had planned and agreed to and did it with grace and love. Their deaths were exactly as they had intended in order to teach me. This book empowered me to open the buried door I worked so hard to avoid and begin walking in my grief.

About the Book

On the night of November 19, 1973, following surgery, thirty-one-year-old wife and mother Betty J. Eadie died.

This is her extraordinary story of the events that followed, her astonishing proof of life after physical death. She saw more, perhaps than any other person has seen before and shares her almost photographic recollections of the remarkable details.

Compelling, inspiring, and infinitely reassuring, her vivid account gives us a glimpse of the peace and unconditional love that awaits us all. More important, Betty's journey offers a simple message that can transform our lives today, showing us our purpose and guiding us to live the way we were meant to—joyously, abundantly, and with love.

Brenda Hennessey, End-of-Life Doula

Brenda resides in a small town in southwestern Ontario. She volunteers at her local residential hospice. Supporting her community is important to Brenda. Being part of a resident's end-of-life journey is an honor and joyous part of her work.

Brenda became an "End-of-Life Doula" in June 2020, completing the certification course through Douglas College. She has since completed palliative care, advanced care planning, MAiD, and grief courses and workshops. Brenda is currently enrolled in the thanatology certificate course through Centennial College. She continues to be an active member of the Death Doula Ontario Network and the Southwestern Ontario Death Doula Network.

Contact Information:
Phone: 519-851-9291
Email: Transitioningtopeace@gmail.com

Reflection Questions for the Reader

What did you like best about this chapter?

_____
_____
_____
_____
_____
_____

What was your favorite passage in this chapter? Why did it stand out?

_____
_____
_____
_____
_____
_____

What feelings did this chapter evoke for you?

_____
_____
_____
_____
_____

If you had the chance to ask the author a question, what would it be?

_____
_____
_____
_____
_____

What form of action does this chapter inspire you to take?

_____
_____
_____
_____
_____

What did you know about this chapter's content before you read it?

___

What new things did you learn from reading this chapter?

___

What questions do you still have?

___

What else have you read on this topic?

_____

_____

_____

_____

_____

_____

Please visit **TenderTruthsCaringForTheDying.com** for more information, including the opportunity to meet the author during an online author and reader gathering.

CHAPTER 6

TENDER TRUTHS OF DYING AND DEATH
Olga Nikolajev

> "All human beings are capable of experiencing
> several different emotions at the same time."
> ~ Dr. Robert Buckman

I am no expert at dying or death. I have not yet died, and I do not know when I will die, but I do know that I will. The truth of our mortality is a given in this life experience. I have dedicated most of my life to thanatology, the study of death, dying, grief, and bereavement. I have been privileged to attend and obtain higher levels of training and education in the field of end-of-life care.

> "Death literacy involves the skills and knowledge
> required to plan for and support ourselves and
> others at the end of life."
> ~ Kathy Kortes-Miller

> *"Death literacy also appears to be a resource that individuals and communities can use for their own benefit strengthening their capacity for future caring."*
> ~ Kerrie Noonan[1]

In my life, I have been present with many forms of dying and death and have experienced many forms of loss and grief. I am a first-generation, Eastern European white female immigrant living in Canada. I have always believed that death is a natural, normal part of life and that we will all experience it uniquely. I recognize and acknowledge my position and stance and my limitations and ignorance in the field of thanatology. I also accept the knowledge I have acquired and gained from my dedication and commitment to the field. I have a filter through which I see the world, a filter through which I see my life experience and attempt to understand the experiences of others as they move through their life, including grief, dying, and death. It's important to be aware of, acknowledge and accept our own filter, how we see the world, and our biased views. By this act of personal truth, we can become aware of and accept our limitations and ignorance.

When we come from a place of vulnerability, not knowing, we can be teachable, curious, and find an empty space inside of ourselves, making space for more awareness and insight. Coming from a place of vulnerability is recognizing that we are stepping into the unknown together. During dying, death, and grief, there is nothing more important than holding an empty sacred space for one another so that we may drop our own truths into the basket of compassion we can weave together.

A fellow co-author in *Bold Spirit Caring for the Dying* quoted an Indigenous Knowledge Keeper saying we are related to everything above and below us.[2] The truth is that we are always in relationship

---

[1] ResearchGate
[2] Wàban, Chrystal, et al. *Bold Spirit Caring for the Dying*. Bold Spirit Press, 2021.

with others, the environment, and the greater physical world, including the spiritual world of the cosmos. Over the years, Indigenous Elders have taught me that we are inter-connected, inter-reliable, and inter-dependent. Our greatest gift in life is caring for life, self, and others with our highest regard, compassion, and care.

Over the last ten years, I have realized through my experiences that dying, death, and grief are relational in nature. When we are dying, we often require a team-based approach to care for us in order to provide support in the various domains of our human experience. Dying, death, and grief require attention to the physical, emotional, psycho-social, and spiritual domains so that this normal and natural process within life can be done with compassion, care, and dignity. Like in birth, we are most vulnerable in our dying and death. In his well-read book *Tuesdays with Morrie*, Mitch Albom shares the words and lived experiences of Morrie Schwartz. Through those stories, we understand better that those who are dying are very vulnerable, seek comfort and support from others, and be held with respect and dignity.[3]

> **"What is a fear of living? It's being pre-eminently afraid of dying. It is not doing what you came here to do, out of timidity and spinelessness. The antidote is to take full responsibility for yourself, for the time you take up and the space you occupy. If you don't know what you're here to do, then just do some good."**
> ~ Maya Angelou

As an end-of-life nurse educator, I have also realized that being present with another's death is a confrontation with our own mortality. As someone who is now, what I consider, in the latter part of my life, I know I am seeking to find my own truth within my own life, including my dying and death. As my family members, friends, and those I care about also come closer to their dying and death, I am reminded of life's

---

[3] Albom, Mitch. *Tuesdays with Morrie*. Crown, 2002.

preciousness and impermanent nature. A known truth is that all things that live will die.

There are many forms of truth. Known truths are often revealed through nature and confirmed by human observation or study. Common truths, which we as a collective of humans agree upon, guide our social order and behavior. Personal truths may be developed based on one's lived experience, and social truths evolve through social interaction and development. The dying process can often reveal our truths as we come to the end of our life and take the chance to be truthful with ourselves, life, and others.

In Dr. David Kuhl's book *Facing Death, Embracing Life,* honesty and truth-telling can often be a catalyst for speaking one's own truth and asking fundamental questions about our own existence and life experience. It is not uncommon for persons at the end of life to ask themselves, "Who am I? What have I done in my life? How have I contributed? Do I have any unfinished business before I die?"[4] These are fundamental questions and go to the heart of our personal truths.

Dying is Natural

One tender truth about caring for the dying is that death is a natural, normal part of our life experience, and we all must come to understand that it is not only the death of a person that creates change and waves of chaos, but all change serves as deaths—ends—that are often followed by a re-birth, and new beginning, and reveal the cyclical nature of life, never really ending. And while we may intellectually understand this tender truth—that death is a natural part of life—we continue to fear the end of our life and all the small deaths in our life because they can fundamentally change and transform us. But natural

---

[4] Kuhl, David. *Facing Death, Embracing Life: Understanding What Dying People Want.* Doubleday Canada, 2006.

dying may sometimes be scary, chaotic, confusing, painful, and traumatic.

One perspective that has helped me accept the truth that death is natural is to accept that everything is always changing. Change is really the only constant in life. From my experience, I have discovered that how I feel right now will not last. I appreciate that my physical body is always in a state of change and that my thoughts are also always changing. Change is neither good nor bad. It just is. In many ways, change gives us the opportunity for something different. It provides us with the understanding that life is constantly in motion and fleeting.

Some see the natural world and the way of nature to be crude and wild, uncontrollable. And nature can absolutely be wild, unpredictable, and sometimes even cruel. But it can also be beautiful, peaceful, and breathtaking. It is similar to the natural dying process.

When you dive deeper into the truth of natural dying, you may find that the physical body enables the dying process to be peaceful and pain-free. As the dying person's body starts to shut down, the mechanisms within render the person no longer hungry or thirsty as they near the end of their life. The changes in the brain, decrease in oxygen, and neurochemistry will often put the person into a deep sleep, a coma, for an extended length of time, where they are no longer aware of their physical body and their environment. But just like entry challenges or difficulties during the birthing process, there are challenges and difficulties in dying.

In hospice palliative care, what is most important is reducing the pain experienced by the dying person. A big part of this approach is addressing the physical pain they may be experiencing from their illness or dying process. Fundamentally end-of-life care services offered in the home, hospital, long-term care, and residential hospices aim to reduce the negative aspect of the natural dying process and alleviate the individual's unique symptoms that the person may experience. At its core, hospice palliative care is an approach to reduce pain and symptoms at the end of life and enhance the comfort and *quality of life* for the person until they die.

So why is the experience of dying and death often painful or confusing? I believe that our current Western culture is far more focused on avoiding dying and death. Some scholars have called this world view "death avoidance" and "death ignorance." Our current world view stems from the effect of medicalization, change in life expectancy, and family dynamics, including caregiving relationships. And even though most are death avoidant, in the Canadian Cardus 2015 report *Death is Natural: Reframing the End-of-Life Conversations in Canada*, the 2013 survey revealed that 75% (majority) of Canadians would prefer to die at home, while only 52% expect this actually to happen.[5] Most of us wish to die at home surrounded by the people we love, those we care for, and those who care for us.

When I think of my own dying and death, I imagine myself at home surrounded by the people who love me, those that can care for me the way I need, wish, and desire. Caring for someone at the end of life often feels like a natural and intuitive process, and caring for them at home feels most comforting. The anxiety and stress carers often feel stems from the lack of knowledge of the dying process, navigating the health care system, and the funeral process. Raising death literacy through death education in communities and providing death education to all who are and will be tasked with caring for the dying will build confidence and skills to reduce the "pain" of dying and death.

Dying is Relational

Death and dying is a relational process and experience. We feel the impact of death on a *personal* level, inside of our being, inside of our psyche, inside of our body, and our emotions. But it is also *relational* in that we are always in relationship with the environment, our support

---

[5] *Death is Natural: Reframing the End-of-Life Conversation in Canada.* Cardus Canada, 2015.

system, caregivers, and family. Our own experiences ripple out and touch the world through our relationships. If we accept the truth that dying and death are relational, we can better understand the cause of pain and suffering for both the person dying and their caregivers.

The dominant assumption in clinical practice is that individuals are autonomous, independent, rational, and hold a high degree of rational decision-making. This assumption is also evident in the field of end-of-life care. But clinicians and social researchers have argued that people's identities, needs, interests, and autonomy are always shared by their relationships with others.[6] This is very true, especially in the care of the dying and the bereaved. After all, dying, death and grief are often seen as life experiences playing out in the social sphere, the intersection between the personal and the social.

End-of-life care and its approach, specifically hospice palliative care, has shifted from an emphasis on the physical aspects of care to a more holistic approach, incorporating the psychosocial and spiritual so that the dying person can be empowered in their living, which includes their dying, until their death.[7]

Respect for one's autonomy is a vital element of end-of-life care in an attempt to provide the highest level of dignity to the individual. The perspective that each person is free to live their life, including their dying and death, independent of outside influences, is a Western post-Enlightenment idea. In Western biomedicine, autonomy is fundamental to one's ability to provide consent and make decisions about care autonomously and independently.

The proponents of individualistic autonomy, especially in medicine, see this as a positive stance that challenges the historical paternalistic approach to care. And while it is important to challenge the "doctor knows best" paradigm, individual autonomy is often easily

---

[6] Dove, E., et al. *Beyond Individualism*, Sage Journals, 2017.
[7] Servaty-Seib, Heather, Chapple, Helen. *The Handbook of Thanatology, Third Edition: The Essential Body of Knowledge for the Study of Death, Dying, and Bereavement.* Association for Death Education and Counseling, 2021.

aligned with existing legal frameworks and principles. In this way, the individual is primarily accountable for their choices and decisions, often releasing the health care provider from responsibility and liability. In addition, this hyper-individualistic perspective feeds into the consumeristic nature of modern health care. Those who criticize the individual autonomy perspective argue that people are rarely "islands onto themselves" and that our identities are always shaped by our relationships with others, including the social structure where these relationships are established and sustained.

While the emergence of *relational autonomy* could address not only an individual's self-determination, it can also incorporate cultural norms where a communal decision-making process occurs. I would argue that we must strive for a relational balance, as some of these collective perspectives could infringe on individual rights and interests. There may not be an easy answer, and the tension between the individual and communal may perpetuate a binary approach, but social research, clinical ethicists, and those at the forefront of end-of-life decision-making are exploring how relational autonomy can be integrated into practice and provide a more holistic framework to bridge together the individual and collective perspectives.

Dying and death is a deeply social process. Not only is our language about dying and death deeply rooted in our cultural and religious contexts, but our death systems are governed by language, economics, and social law. Approaches to the care of the dying and the dead are different worldwide, illustrating that different forms of death systems are covered by different ideals about individual autonomy.

Dying is Holistic

Mental Aspect

Physical Aspect **Sexual Aspect** **Spiritual Aspect**

Emotional Aspect

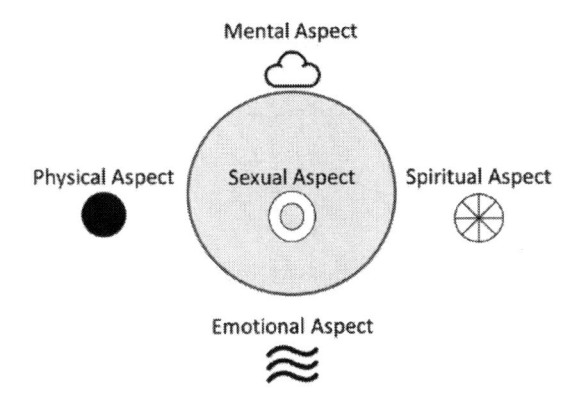

Figure 1 Image Source: Orsi, 1999

Another tender truth is that dying, death, and grief are holistic. A holistic perspective acknowledges that humans are complex and that we are multidimensional, having several aspects to being human. We have emotional, physical, mental, spiritual, and psychosocial aspects. The holistic framework and approach to the care of the dying were initially introduced by Dame Cecil Saunders (1967), considered the grandmother of the modern hospice movement. Saunders introduced us to the concept of "total pain," whereby those providing support were encouraged to address the physical, emotional, psychosocial, and existential suffering that the dying person may experience during their end-of-life experience.

I have conceded that my personal identity has many aspects. I have emotional, physical, mental, spiritual, and sexual aspects of self that I experience within a particular cultural and social landscape, my family, my community, and where I live. My emotional self and development are tied to my family and the emotional mirroring and validation I received from childhood into adulthood. I have come to better understand my emotional self through study and life experience. From some of my shamanic teachings, I have seen my emotions like energy in motion, like water, always changing, moving, and transforming. Through mindfulness, I have witnessed my many emotional states and their origin and how I may be able to move through some of the most intense feelings, such as grief. Our physical body is like the earth, like the soil, plants, and animals, like nature, constantly changing, moving, and transforming. The mental aspect of self, through the shamanic perspective, is seen as clouds, wind, fleeting, and always changing. And our spiritual aspect is like the element of fire, which often brings us hope and determination. When I align myself with the elements, I feel and appreciate myself as part of the natural world. Death is not the opposite of life, it is the opposite of birth, and life is forever changing and transforming between our entry (birth) and exit (death).

When we acknowledge that death and the dying process are natural, relational, and holistic, we can better understand some of the pains, discomforts, and uneasiness that we may experience as we care for those dying and grieving and approach death ourselves.

Now that we recognize dying and death as a natural, relational, and holistic process, let's turn to the "difficulties" or "pains" of dying and death. While we can find stories and narratives of those who have died contributing to our awareness of some possible aspects, much of our personal experience of death is unknown because we have yet to experience it. The fear of the unknown often becomes the first pain that we may feel. The endless questions we may have about the process, how much time we have, how it will happen, what we may be able to control, and what we will not have any control over can spin us into deep death anxiety and uncertainty. With all of these questions, we may spiral into confusion and despair.

The stress and pain of the unknown are also experienced by those in relationship with the person dying. Their own understanding and experience of being with dying and death inform their approach and belief of the experience. Companioning and being fully present without judgment with the dying and those caring for them is key in reducing the stress of the pain of the unknown. When those caring for the dying are able to make space for conversations about the unknown, the dying and those caring for them have an opportunity to better identify their fears, wishes, desires, and needs that can be helpful to ease the pain and stress. When the dying person has a better understanding of what they may experience, their stress is reduced, and they are able to bring meaning to their experience. As relational and social beings, we often feel better when our experience is witnessed and validated, without judgment but with compassion and care.

Open communication is key in reducing death anxiety. Truth-telling must be part of this communication to better prepare for what we may experience or what we can anticipate at the end of life. When those dying are not told what is happening or what they may experience, there is a risk that they will not be able to say what they need or wish to say to those in their circle, those they are in relationship with. One important aspect of sharing our thoughts, stories, and experiences is knowing we are not alone. It is one way that we can overcome our feelings of isolation.

Those dying may also experience physical, emotional, and spiritual pain. I believe that part of this painful experience is the way of dying, how we must "separate" from our body, our environment, and those we care about.

When my mother was very, very sick, sick enough to die, I thought about her dying. I experienced anticipatory grief as I contemplated her dying and death, the end of our physical relationship. I could feel the pain of that possible separation, emotionally and physically. As I anticipated losing her, I felt the pain in my body, in my heart. I felt the pain of that separation, and my mind raced to try to find logical ways that I could bring some comfort to myself.

I think of the pains of dying as the contractions of labor, the contractions and expansions, the breathing in and breathing out. And like the birthing process, caregivers can provide education, information, and comfort during a very chaotic time. Because dying is holistic and relational, it requires a multi-disciplinary approach to care so that all aspects of the personal and collective experience can be supported.

REFERENCES

Albom, Mitch. (2017). *Tuesdays with Morrie.* New York, New York: Broadway Books.

Kortes-Miller, K. (2018). *Talking about death won't kill you: The essential guide to end-of-life conversations.* Toronto, Ontario, Canada: ECW Press.

Kuhl, David. (2006) *Facing Death, Embracing Life.* Toronto, Ontario: Doubleday Canada.

Lux, Tamelynda, et al. (2021) *Bold Spirit Caring for the Dying.* London, Ontario: Bold Spirit Press.

Strikes, Thunder, et al. (1999) Song of the Deer. Scottsdale, AZ: Prizm Productions Inc.

୫୦ ଔ

Self-Care Tip

You cannot give from an empty cup.

The primary self-care tip I can give you is to not approach self-care as something you do *after* you have exhausted yourself. Self-care needs to be an ongoing practice, a process that you engage in daily to maintain self-resilience and resolve. Start with an easy practice technique such as mindful breathing and build upon the tools and techniques that work best for you. Many end-of-life care practitioners and caregivers think self-care is selfish, and their focus must always be on caregiving. If you can imagine that we have only a finite amount of energy, how we spend that energy, protect it, and build our reserves back up again is important. Self-care can be as simple as saying "no" to others when you need to focus on yourself. Creating healthy boundaries is not always easy to do but is vitally important in protecting your personal space and energy.

A Quote That Inspires

"All human beings are capable of experiencing several different emotions at the same time," wrote Dr. Robert Buckman in his book *I Don't Know What to Say: How to Help and Support Someone Who is Dying*. This quote speaks to the quantum physics of end-of-life care and our human ability to experience all of our emotions, sometimes simultaneously. That is often why our grief and mourning are so confusing to us and others because we can "switch" between these emotions. This experience often feels confusing and chaotic for the griever and those caring for them as we attempt to stabilize or bring clarity to our emotional states.

One Tip or Strategy to Help Others

I encourage caregivers to care for themselves not as a reward but as a needed practice to maintain and sustain their resilience and energy. Another tip I would like to suggest, especially to those that provide end-of-life care services, is to be willing to accept assistance and help from others. Those who care for others often do not seek support or help because they think they "should" be able to care for themselves. When it comes time to care for my own parents, I need to be their daughter, not their end-of-life practitioner. I anticipate that I will be surprised by my own grief and may not be "clear-headed" to think of all the practical things that may need to be taken care of. So, if you are caring for your own family, take the time to BE present without the pressure to always BE in your role as a caregiver. And if you find that you may be limited in the professional support you need, please ensure that you have a friend and/or colleague who is willing to listen and offer support to you.

Something I Wish I'd Known When I Began This Journey as a Practitioner in End-of-Life Care and What I Discovered

One thing I wish I had known before beginning this journey in end-of-life care and death education is how personally it will impact me. I not only spent time professionally engaging in thanatology, the study of death, dying, loss and grief, but I also spent a lot of my time contemplating, reflecting on, and exploring how I feel and think about my own dying, death, and grief. This includes those in my immediate environment. I am also now deeply aware that my life's "work" impacts those around me, not always positively. I am now more aware of how my work affects my mood and emotional and mental health. That is why it is so vital to have a brave space for me to discuss and debrief my experiences as an end-of-life practitioner and/or death educator.

ಸಿ ಣ

> **"Being present to another person's pain; it is not about taking away the pain."**
> ~ Dr. Wolfelt, *Companioning the Bereaved*

There's something about the tension between holding the bigger space without judgment or agendas for another person as they experience pain. How do we describe pain? Dame Cecile Saunders talks about total pain—physical, psychosocial, and spiritual—that people experience.

The truth is that it's difficult to sit with somebody else's pain, especially if attempting to create a space that is void of judgment or evaluation so that they can process whatever is happening. Where is the pain? What kind of pain are they feeling? The tender truth is that it's difficult because maybe not in the moment, but certainly afterward, I reflect on that experience that I was a witness to. Sometimes I feel the pain inside because I can only imagine what it's like. So, if they're having a painful experience in maybe a conversation about the fact that they're leaving the people they care about, I reflect on that experience and how it may be true for me as well.

People will feel these different kinds of pains, and they will impact us. Their experience speaks to what we may experience ourselves. If I want the knowledge, the power of that moment, then I will be impacted by it. There's an opportunity to learn. How am I in my relationship with others? Do they pain me? Do I have physical pain? How am I caring for my physical well-being?

I am thankful for the opportunities that I have had and the privilege of being at the bedside as a nurse, and I do the best I can to reduce some of that pain, whether physical, social, or spiritual.

The tender truth is that end of life can be painful. It may not have physical pain, but you may have some experience with the pain of withdrawing or separation. An energetic separation can cause pain due to the endings of things, the endings of stories. It's like a contraction, a labor pain, as we experience the leaving, leaving our current life reality.

The big piece for me that has always been and continues to be an important part of caring for the dying is personal self-care. The tender truth of caregiving is that you must put your mask on first. I don't know who said it first, and I'm not going to be the only person and the last person to say it, but there is an understanding that when we care for others, we need to take care of ourselves. Fundamentally I would coach or guide new end-of-life care practitioners to discover their capacity for care and how to take care of themselves as they provide support to others. We have levels of capacity. And we have the capacity for caring from our different aspects. We can best provide physical, emotional, mental, and spiritual support to others when we have capacity. And sometimes, we may not have the capacity at all.

Therefore, we need to be self-aware of our needs and how we build our capacity to care. So much of being an effective caregiver for those at the end of life is about our self-awareness, understanding our capacity, and how we impact others when we don't have the capacity to care.

In end-of-life doula training, I speak about the different kinds of death experiences. When faced with a traumatic, very energy-consuming situation with a lot of uncertainty and chaos, it is especially important to be at full capacity in all aspects to support others during this chaotic time.

In *Bold Spirit Caring for the Dying* (2021), I invite the reader to engage in a death awareness meditation, but I encourage the reader to skip the exercise if they do not feel comfortable. I mention that so they're not placed into a really difficult or challenging position. Having said that, I also know from my nursing experiences and other life experiences that the greatest learning was in my ability to hold a neutral healing space for someone else even when I didn't think that I had the ability to do so. I learned through those times when I almost thought my capacity cup would break, to understand the depth or volume of my capacity during very challenging times.

The pandemic created a lot of challenges for many, including myself, both professionally and personally, but I was able to "hold it together" because I had the support of a caring circle, gathering together with others who were caring for themselves and others. The circle enabled me to seal up some of the cracks in my cup. I think this is what Dr. Gabor Maté means in relation to resilience being a social quality, not so much an individual quality. In order for my cup to have stayed together, it was held by the glue of my caring circle.

Actually, I don't even know if my cup broke. It may have broken or cracked open, but it landed in the basket of a caring circle.

Additional Question Asked by Interviewer: *There seem to be end-of-life doulas stuck in the grief of a particular loss, and as they attempt to practice as an end-of-life practitioner in whatever role they're in, they're still working through their own grief. Some bring their bias from their own world into whatever's happening in the moment with a client or client's family. Some might even say, "Honestly, you shouldn't be a practitioner because you are not healed. You are not well enough. You're doing this to help you heal." Or "You're not ready to be an end-of-life practitioner." We sometimes judge ourselves and ask if we are ready to be end-of-life practitioners. What insight can you offer as a veteran end-of-life practitioner?*

It's helpful to unpack it. If I unpack it, then are we assuming that only those who are healed, whatever that means, can then heal others?

As an end-of-life practitioner, I need to make sure that I can either remove myself (physically or mentally) or create more distance from a given situation to process how it's infiltrating or impacting my space.

There is a risk that many of those learning how to do this work may overstep. They sometimes overstep because if we know that not knowing can be hurtful and harmful to people, then we want to ensure that those who are leading and those who are supporting at least have a grounded sense of the basic principles, fundamental responsibilities, and ethics—what it means to be an end-of-life care practitioner. And I hope that I have conveyed that to them in my dissemination of information as an end-of-life doula instructor. But I also recognize that I'm not able to control how people update their knowledge and how they take on the particular role.

I strongly suggest that end-of-life practitioners have the emotional and mental intelligence to understand their role, limitations, and ethical responsibilities. Even informal caregivers have ethical responsibilities.

This brings me back to the original insight about the cup being past capacity and beginning to break. Let's talk about another tender truth that has just come up. There can be an instance, an assignment, a moment to time, a client where we are past capacity and truly breaking, and actually find that we cannot hold it together.

For an end-of-life practitioner, in that instance, it's about transparency from the beginning. When working with the client's family, I do my best to not make promises or influence the outcome. I'm not the expert. I have to take care of myself to be at the bedside and provide support from my cup that has not run over or is on the verge of breaking. We need to know and anticipate the stress and workload so we don't get to that breaking point. And if it does happen, then it's about meeting the situation with honesty, integrity, and transparency.

There have been times when I couldn't anticipate the things I would see or how I would respond based on the situation. And in the moment, that's probably where my cup was about to crack, and I could say to myself, *Okay, hold on a second. Let me get grounded. I'm going to set myself aside a little bit and be with this person who this is happening to. It's not happening to me. It's happening to them.* And then I have to recover and not allow the trauma to stick. I would cry, shake, dance, or sing to bring myself back to a well-balanced grounded sense of self.

End-of-life practitioners need to take care of themselves and know the tools or techniques to remove the tension from the body and their mind, recover and lean in to providing support. I ask people who need support: What do you need? Do you need comfort? Do you need a strategy to work through something? Or do you not need to pay attention to it and find some form of distraction?

It's about that relational autonomy because we have been taught to care for others, life, and self. We must take care of ourselves first, then our life and others. It is NOT selfish to care for yourself before you care for others.

We also talk about how do you prepare? What's your mantra? What's your zip-up? What's your cloak? What's your way that you can be in a space that is very chaotic, very turbulent, very confusing and uncertain, and changing all the time? How can you be the eye in the storm? And then how do you recover from that particular experience?

How do you ground yourself? How do you put your feet on the ground—sing, resonate, dance, be physical, cry.

We also must acknowledge that our recovery needs to be ritual. If your trauma happens in a specific intensity of experience, then I don't want to re-traumatize you, but negative experiences can heal by going back energetically and shifting the perception of that experience.

Book Recommended by Olga Nikolajev

I Don't Know What to Say:
How to Help and Support Someone Who is Dying
~ Dr. Robert Buckman

Dr. Buckman shares his professional experiences caring for those at the end of life and informs us, the reader, that we can learn the skills to listen better and be present for those that are dying and grieving. He illustrates why it's important to listen and talk to those who are dying and grieving and offers suggestions for starting and maintaining the often intimate and tender conversations. He also covers topics such as active, sensitive listening, explains the dying process, and offers insight into the process of grief and how we may be able to support ourselves and others through the recovery and healing through grief.

The book impacted me deeply as I read the various and touching dying and caring experiences. It allowed me to better understand the limits of my nursing training and ignited in me a deep curiosity to learn more about the end-of-life process and how I could contribute in a way that was holistic and relational.

About the Book

When faced with a dying person, the combination of fear, embarrassment, guilt, and profound sadness can make the most caring person feel helpless. For many of us, dying is so far removed from everyday experience that we just don't know what to do.

Knowing how to listen sensitively and knowing what to say to a dying person can help make this a moving and rewarding time for patient and supporter.

Book Recommended by Olga Nikolajev

Facing Death, Embracing Life: Understanding What Dying People Want
~ Dr. David Kuhl

Dr. Kuhl offers insights into the tension of time and anxiety for the person who is dying and those who accompany them. His book not only offers suggestions from his professional and personal experiences but also offers self-reflection and meditation and encourages readers to engage in a reflective practice as they contemplate death, dying, and grief. You will have a chance to learn throughout the book about how to "break bad news," cope and manage pain, and offers suggestions on how we may navigate the tender truths of unfinished business and our life review.

This book impacted my ability to better serve those that I am working with and enabled me to see that end-of-life care has the potential for healing our relationships, our life experiences, and the way we approach life, including dying, death, and grief.

About the Book

A practical and compassionate guide to living with a terminal illness, written by a well-respected palliative care doctor.

In his highly regarded bestseller What Dying People Want, Dr. David Kuhl provided valuable insights into the experience of living with a terminal illness. In this guide, Dr. Kuhl distills the practical advice he presented in his first book and helps readers to cope with a terminal illness by providing concrete, step-by-step suggestions, as well as offering space for private reflection. This format will allow readers — those contending with terminal illness as well as their family and friends — to sort through difficult but vital conversations with loved ones and caregivers before they take place.

This guide includes advice on:
- Talking to health care providers about treatment and diagnosis
- Learning the right questions to ask specialists
- Finding out about alternative treatments

TENDER TRUTHS CARING FOR THE DYING

- Considering home care vs. hospitalization
- Finding sources of financial support
- Offering space and guidance for recording and reflecting on larger, more emotional themes

Olga Nikolajev, RN, MA, FT

Olga Nikolajev is an end-of-life nurse educator, cannabis nurse educator, and end-of-life doula mentor with over twenty-five years of professional experience as a registered nurse in various health care settings, including hospice palliative care. Olga has been involved in national, provincial, and local community efforts to shift how we view and approach our dying experience, death, and grief. She serves as the elected International Representative and Council Secretary on the Credentialing Council of the Association of Death Education and Counseling (ADEC). Olga facilitates courses in thanatology and end-of-life doula across Canada. Olga is the founder and director of Dying Matters, death awareness and educational social enterprise, and the Death Doula Ontario Network, which she founded in June 2020.

Contact Information:
Email: onikolajev1970@gmail.com
Website: www.dyingmatters.ca
Website: www.deathdoulaontarionetwork.ca

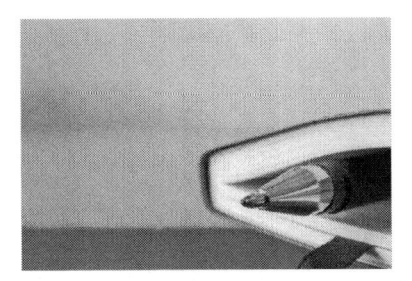

Reflection Questions for the Reader

What did you like best about this chapter?

_____
_____
_____
_____
_____

What was your favorite passage in this chapter? Why did it stand out?

_____
_____
_____
_____
_____

What feelings did this chapter evoke for you?

If you had the chance to ask the author a question, what would it be?

What form of action does this chapter inspire you to take?

What did you know about this chapter's content before you read it?

What new things did you learn from reading this chapter?

What questions do you still have?

What else have you read on this topic?

_____

_____

_____

_____

_____

_____

Please visit **TenderTruthsCaringForTheDying.com** for more information, including the opportunity to meet the author during an online author and reader gathering.

CO-AUTHOR DIALOGUE

i

Q: **We cannot work with all clients. What limits and boundaries do you have that would mean referring to another professional?**

Responses:

As a chaplain (and an ordained minister), there are certain ethical considerations that mandate I refer to another professional (as is the case with most - if not all - helping professions).

Since end-of-life and grief work are the most intimate types of caring for someone, the same boundaries I have as a clinical hypnotist are different from my work as a chaplain or minister.

However, there are definitive guidelines that require I refer to a professional. Whenever counseling goes beyond spiritual understanding, I refer to an appropriate licensed counselor.

~ Rusty Williams

In my role as an end-of-life doula and hospice volunteer, I am mindful of my scope of practice. I am a companion to the dying and the grieving by sitting with them, providing comfort in their physical surroundings, listening to their stories, and holding space for them. When questions, requests, or choices are outside my scope of practice, a referral to another professional is necessary. Perhaps it may be one of the medical team members at the hospice or connecting them to support through a religious belief organization.

~ Brenda Hennessey

Some professional, caring, and personal limitations and boundaries are important. The key for me is being aware of the limits and boundaries of my professional practice by being transparent and even stating that I may need to refer for more or specialized support. I encourage other end-of-life practitioners to continue to deepen their understanding of their limitations based on the scope of practice and their own emotional, physical, mental, and spiritual capacity. We **cannot** be the **only** caregivers and supporters for a client family.

~ Olga Nikolajev

Reader's Insights & Takeaways:

_____
_____
_____
_____
_____
_____
_____
_____

Q: Have you encountered disenfranchised or complicated grief? What did it look like, and how did you offer support?

Responses:

The most common type of disenfranchised grief I've encountered is when a family pet dies. The family is hurting, and they might hear things like: "It was only a pet; it's not like you lost a parent."

This adds to the pain, and when I've witnessed it, I've made sure to comfort the grieving family and remind them that grief is grief, and no one has the right to dictate when or how a person grieves. I also remind them that whatever they are feeling is normal and encourage them to be gentle with themselves.

If the situation warrants it, I might share my experience(s) of losing a pet. I mention the pain I felt and how I had many emotions. This is the "me too" moment when the other person feels like they aren't alone in what they are going through.

I've also been called to comfort the parents of a child who died in utero. A couple dear to us experienced this last year. Well-intentioned friends told them that they are young and could try again. Worse advice was given, but I'll spare everyone what was said.

In situations when parents lose a child in the womb, I don't say much - I just listen and remind them that they are not alone. This is one of those times when I might refer out to a professional trained for this type of loss.

~ Rusty Williams

Yes, I have provided support for people experiencing complicated or disenfranchised grief. I have observed their struggle to "come to terms with" what has happened, often disappointed by support from others, their partner, their family, and their community. The best I have offered is my undivided attention to them sharing their experience with their struggles to find balance and some sense of okay-ness with the world. A loss that is not deemed "important" by society or has limitations on its grieving can spin a person into experiencing this type of grieving, where they often feel a sense of loss of control, loss of "what could have been," loss of the "way life is to be."

~ Olga Nikolajev

As a social worker and grief counselor, I have encountered many clients who have experienced disenfranchised or complicated grief.

First, meeting where the client is at is vital. Do they need help with practical matters such as activities of daily living? Learning what supports they have. How they have navigated stressful moments in life in the past. What are their strengths, how can we engage these, and what isn't working?

Validating their feelings and allowing them to feel heard is also essential. Listening to their stories, especially when associated with disenfranchised grief, they already think unheard of by the people around them and society.

Give them time. Do not hurry the person to "work through" and find closure. Grief is a process. It takes time and understanding. There is no closure grief never ends. Truly the goal is to make it not so overwhelming and heavy to carry.

~ Patti Broadfoot

Reader's Insights & Takeaways:

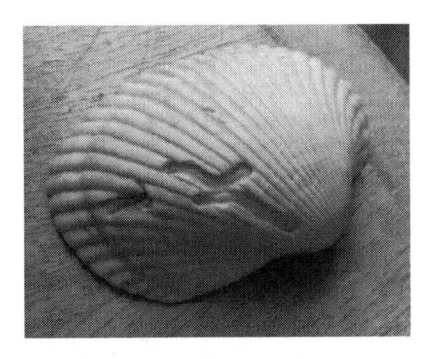

Q: What do you do to prepare yourself for questions that might/will come from a dying person when you are with them (prayer, meditation, research, listening to music, etc.)? How do you center yourself in order to be able to be both compassionate and honest when asked difficult questions from the dying or from their loved ones?

Responses:

Develop a self-care practice: mantra, deep breathing, centering, shielding, shedding, and debriefing. Also, set realistic expectations of yourself, set good professional and personal boundaries, and understand your limits.

~ Olga Nikolajev

I take a deep breath and do my best to pause and also do my best to remain curious and open.

~ Tamelynda Lux

A devoted self-care practice is crucial. It helps to reduce anxiety and stress and really keeps you mentally healthy. Additionally, regularly practicing mindfulness (such as deep breathing, meditation, etc.) creates a procedural memory that you can connect with quicker when met with a stressful moment, being asked difficult questions from the dying or their loved ones.

Secondly, knowing my boundaries and limitations. Both professionally and personally. I can be knowledgeable about death and dying and learn about the client's ideas and wishes, but I also recognize that I'm not the expert. The client is the expert. I am always curious about why the difficult questions are being asked. I think of it like following a breadcrumb trail of their thoughts and fears. I often find they are really wrestling with the answer that it is often a reality they are trying themselves to process. Asking open-ended questions led by a breadcrumb trail of what they share with me allows them to come to a conclusion or answer within themselves.

~ Patti Broadfoot

Being a spiritual person, it's important for me to ask for guidance and ground myself before spending time at the hospice. I have a little prayer I do before entering the residence that helps me to stay in the present moment. Being open to their questions, listening with a non-judgemental heart, and being honest with my answers is very the best way I can support and provide comfort to the dying and/or their loved ones.

~ Brenda Hennessey

CO-AUTHOR DIALOGUE

Reader's Insights & Takeaways:

Q: When did you realize that talking about death at the dinner table with your partner and/or family was becoming normal?

Responses:

My 26-year-old son said to me one day – "mom, why do you always talk about death?". My response to him was that it would happen to all of us at some point, so it's best to talk about it now rather than later. That was the day I realized that I speak about it a lot as it's part of my everyday life.

~ Brenda Hennessey

When my partner or parents brought up the topic, and we had a lovely discussion.

~ Olga Nikolajev

When I took my first course as an end-of-life doula, I would come home and tell my spouse about all the things I had learned that day and how they "fit" or didn't fit with my lived experience. My family never spoke about death at any time, let alone at the dinner table, even when my grandmother was dying.

~ Tamelynda Lux

TENDER TRUTHS CARING FOR THE DYING

Reader's Insights & Takeaways:

Q: How do you continue to integrate new information and knowledge into your practice? And how are you "grounding" your new insights and awareness?

What I have observed and experienced is that the landscape of end-of-life care continues to evolve and shift, as we have seen with Medical Assistance in Dying (MAID) legislation in Canada. For those of us who are death educators, how do we ensure that death education continues to grow and evolve and include new areas of interest and social changes?

Responses:

Reading and research. I also look for courses that are relevant to my work. I am nearing the end of a train-the-trainer program for an organization that teaches resiliency skills around the country. Much of what is in the course applies to chaplaincy work (and, by extension, caring for the dying and their loved ones).

~ Rusty Williams

I continue to read new literature related to grief research, thanatology, and end-of-life care. I am fortunate that I get to educate and lead others in this field because it gives me the opportunity to continue my own learning from a professional and personal level. My networks and associations are also a good source of updated and new information and knowledge, a collective mind. I also practice humility and remind myself that I will NEVER know everything and that my students and client families are the greatest source of my learning.

~ Olga Nikolajev

I'm reading. I also participate in a number of Facebook groups to learn more about how others are feeling and doing through their journeys. For grounding, I am part a client of the Alzheimer's Society and attend support groups; I have a social worker who I can call when needed for additional support.

~ Tamelynda Lux

I am a learning nerd. The more learning, the better. I have always felt that the minute I'm not learning (especially with EBP's), my clients aren't learning and growing too.

~ Patti Broadfoot

I believe we will spend our entire life learning personally and professionally. Spending time with hospice residents and peers provides new information and knowledge each day. We are blessed to have the technology that allows us to share information shared by various organizations focusing on end-of-life care and support. For example, the Death Doula Ontario Network provides a community of sharing resources, hosting training workshops, and members give personal support to other doulas and me through meetings and connections.

As I learn new insights and awareness, it's important to be open-minded and allow the learnings to flow naturally into conversations with those I'm serving. For example, a resident in the hospice was sharing with me that she did not wish to be buried in the ground yet was very scared of cremation because a fire had destroyed their family home when she was a child. I provided information regarding Aquamation as another choice or option for her. She was so relieved to hear about this process and began discussing it with her family immediately. As I reflected on this situation, she had a sense of excitement when informing her family of this option. This awareness reduced her fears associated with burial and cremation by fire.

~ Brenda Hennessey

Reader's Insights & Takeaways:

_____

_____

_____

_____

_____

_____

_____

_____

Dr. Alan Wolfelt's
Eleven Tenets of Companioning the Bereaved
by Center for Loss

1. Companioning is about being present to another person's pain; it is not about taking away the pain.
2. Companioning is about going to the wilderness of the soul with another human being;

   it is not about thinking you are responsible for finding the way out.
3. Companioning is about honoring the spirit;

   it is not about focusing on the intellect.
4. Companioning is about listening with the heart;

   it is not about analyzing with the head.
5. Companioning is about bearing witness to the struggles of others;

   it is not about judging or directing these struggles.
6. Companioning is about walking alongside;

   it is not about leading.
7. Companioning is about discovering the gifts of sacred silence;

   it is not about filling up every moment with words.
8. Companioning is about being still;

   it is not about frantic movement.
9. Companioning is about respecting disorder and confusion;

   it is not about imposing order and logic.
10. Companioning is about learning from others;

    it is not about teaching them.
11. Companioning is about compassionate curiosity;

    it is not about expertise.

~ Reprinted with permission: **www.centerforloss.com**

CONTACT INFORMATION

Patti Broadfoot – Chapter 1
Phone: 226-270-5028
Email: Info@innersojourn.net
Website: innersojourn.net

Brenda Hennessey – Chapter 5
Phone: 519-851-9291
Email: Transitioningtopeace@gmail.com

Tamelynda Lux – Chapter 4
Phone: 519-670-5219
Email: info@TamelyndaLux.com
Website: TamelyndaLux.com ~and~ StepStoneHypnosis.com
Mailing: PO Box 29061, London, Ontario N6K 4L9 Canada

Olga Nikolajev – Chapter 6
Email: onikolajev1970@gmail.com
Website: www.dyingmatters.ca
Website: deathdoulaontarionetwork.ca

Chrystal Waban Toop – Chapter 2
Email: blackbirdmedicines@gmail.com
Website: blackbirdmedicines.ca ~and~ ogimakwe.com

Rusty Williams – Chapter 3
Phone: 609-975-8420
Email: 13.RWilliams@gmail.com
Website: TheBarefootMinistries.org

ABOUT TAMELYNDA LUX
as Project Lead and Publisher

My name is Tamelynda Lux. I am an author, editor, book coach, and publishing project manager.

For over three decades, I have invested my career supporting individuals as a life coach and evolved my private practice to include hypnosis for life issues and concerns. Editing has been a paid hobby for over thirty years, and when the pandemic hit in 2020, it became much more than just a hobby. With all of my combined expertise, I bring a perspective that empowers authors to explore and connect even more deeply to their work, enhancing and showcasing their passion through their writing. This makes my work with authors distinctive.

I always had a book inside of me, thinking one day I would write that book. I procrastinated for over a decade, but with a coach and accountability partner, it only took one month of focused writing and another couple of months to edit, format, and publish it. My first book made it in time for my fiftieth birthday! What a day it was as I held my first book in my hands, seeing my ideas in print and my name and photograph on the book. To say I felt excited, energized, and triumphant doesn't even begin to describe how I felt. My birthday party and book launch was one of the best celebrations ever!

Fast forward to 2020, and I wanted to write a book on a relatively new topic but didn't think I had enough content to fill a book. And I didn't want to procrastinate for another decade. That's when I decided to write just one chapter and invite others to join me in writing a book.

You, too, can become a published author. I will guide and coach you. For more information, please contact me: info@TamelyndaLux.com.

"Success comes in cans, not can'ts."

~ Brian Tracy

MORE ABOUT THIS BOOK

Website: www.CaringForTheDyingBook.com

Email: info@CaringForTheDyingBook.com

Facebook: @BoldSpiritCaringForTheDyingBook

Please Leave a Review on Amazon

because it can help other practitioners and caregivers decide this is a book for them to read while on their journey of providing end-of-life care.

~ **Thank you.** ~

If you are interested in participating as
a co-author in a future project,
please contact Tamelynda Lux at:
info@TamelyndaLux.com

Tamelynda Lux is available for podcasts
and other speaking engagements.

Please contact:
info@TamelyndaLux.com

ABOUT BOLD SPIRIT PRESS

Tamelynda Lux, Founder/Owner
PO Box 29061, London, Ontario Canada N6K 4L9
(519) 670-5219

www.BoldSpiritPress.com
info@BoldSpiritPress.com

**Are you interested in
sharing an experience and becoming a
co-author in a future book?**
Many topics are being considered.

Contact me!

Manufactured by Amazon.ca
Bolton, ON

31245960R00107